SEP 3 0 2013

MUSICIANS
OF THE
RENAISSANCE

THE RENAISSANCE

MUSICIANS OF THE RENAISSANCE

Edited by Kathleen Kuiper, Senior Editor, Arts and Culture

Glenview Public Library
1930 GLENVIEW ROAD
GLENVIEW, ILLINOIS 60025
847-729-7500

Britannica
Educational Publishing

IN ASSOCIATION WITH

ROSEN
EDUCATIONAL SERVICES

Published in 2013 by Britannica Educational Publishing
(a trademark of Encyclopædia Britannica, Inc.) in association with Rosen Educational
Services, LLC

29 East 21st Street, New York, NY 10010.

Copyright © 2013 Encyclopædia Britannica, Inc. Britannica, Encyclopædia Britannica,
and the Thistle logo are registered trademarks of Encyclopædia Britannica, Inc. All
rights reserved.

Rosen Educational Services materials copyright © 2013 Rosen Educational Services, LLC.
All rights reserved.

Distributed exclusively by Rosen Educational Services.
For a listing of additional Britannica Educational Publishing titles, call toll free (800) 237-9932.

First Edition

Britannica Educational Publishing
J.E. Luebering: Senior Manager
Marilyn L. Barton: Senior Coordinator, Production Control
Steven Bosco: Director, Editorial Technologies
Lisa S. Braucher: Senior Producer and Data Editor
Yvette Charboneau: Senior Copy Editor
Kathy Nakamura: Manager, Media Acquisition
Kathleen Kuiper, Senior Editor, Arts and Culture

Rosen Educational Services
Jeanne Nagle: Senior Editor
Nelson Sá: Art Director
Cindy Reiman: Photography Manager
Brian Garvey: Designer, Cover Design
Introduction by Laura Loria

Library of Congress Cataloging-in-Publication Data

Musicians of the Renaissance/edited by Kathleen Kuiper.—1st ed.
    p. cm.—(The Renaissance)
"In association with Britannica Educational Publishing, Rosen Educational Services."
Includes bibliographical references and index.
ISBN 978-1-61530-878-1 (library binding)
1. Composers—Biography. 2. Music—15th century—History and criticism. 3. Music—16th
century—History and criticism. 4. Music—17th century—History and criticism. I. Kuiper,
Kathleen.
ML390.M959 2013
780.9'031—dc23

                                                                    2012024845

Manufactured in the United States of America

On the cover, p. iii: Portrait of Claudio Monteverdi. *Imagno/Hulton Archive/Getty Images*

Cover (background pattern), pp. i, iii, 1, 28, 49, 67, 100, 125, 145, 147, 149 © iStockphoto.
com/fotozambra; p. x (sun) Hemera/Thinkstock; remaining interior graphic elements ©
iStockphoto.com/Petr Babkin

CONTENTS

Introduction	x
Chapter 1: The Transition to the Renaissance	1
Development of Polyphony	3
Guido d'Arezzo	5
The Notre-Dame School	6
Ars Nova	8
Ars Antiqua	9
Monophonic Secular Song	10
The Early Renaissance	13
The Court of Burgundy	14
New Religious Musical Forms	15
Secular Music	15
The Franco-Flemish School	16
Instrumental Music	18
Musical Forms	19
Toccata	20
Solo and Ensemble Instruments	22
Renaissance Vocal Music	23
Italy	25
England	26
France	27
Germany and Other Areas of Europe	27
Chapter 2: Renaissance Musical Instruments	28
Lute	28

Other Stringed Instruments 31
   Theorbo 31
   Rebec 33
   Viol 33
   Percussion Instruments 35
Organ 37
Stringed Keyboard Instruments 38
   Clavichord 40
   Harpsichord 42
   Spinet 42
   Psaltery 43
   Virginal 44
   Assorted Wind Instruments 45
   Serpent 46

Chapter 3: Early Renaissance Composers 49
   John Dunstable 49
   Guillaume Dufay 50
   Chanson 51
   Binchois 54
   Jean de Ockeghem 55
   Jakob Obrecht 57
   Josquin des Prez 58
   Counterpoint in the Renaissance 61
   Heinrich Isaac 62
   Loyset Compère 63

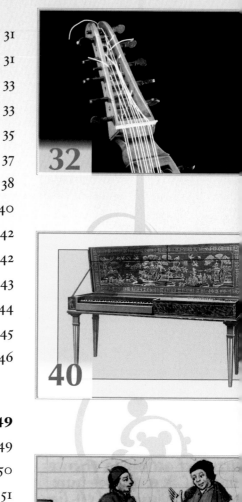

Pierre de La Rue 64

Jean Mouton 65

Chapter 4: Later Renaissance Composers Active in Italy 67

Jacques Arcadelt 67

    Frottole 68

Philippe de Monte 69

Orlando di Lasso 71

Giaches de Wert 73

Luca Marenzio 74

Carlo Gesualdo, principe di Venosa, conte di Conza 75

    Renaissance Music Printers 78

Giovanni Pierluigi da Palestrina 80

    Life 80

    Music 84

Andrea Gabrieli 87

Giovanni Gabrieli 88

Claudio Monteverdi 89

    The Gonzaga Court 91

    Three Decades in Venice 95

Chapter 5: Later Renaissance Composers Active in England 100

Robert Fayrfax 100

John Taverner 101

Christopher Tye 102

Thomas Tallis   103

  Fitzwilliam Virginal Book   105

William Byrd   106

  Life   106

  Legacy   109

Thomas Morley   110

John Dowland   112

John Bull   113

John Wilbye   115

Thomas Campion   116

  Ayre   117

Francis Pilkington   119

Thomas Weelkes   120

Robert Johnson   121

Orlando Gibbons   122

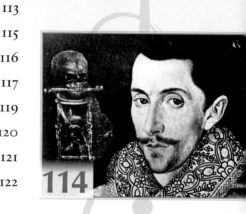

Chapter 6: Later Renaissance Composers Active in Other Countries

Chapter 6: Later Renaissance
Composers Active in Other
Countries   **125**

Clément Janequin   125

Claudin de Sermisy   126

  The Genevan Psalter   127

Loys Bourgeois   127

Claude Goudimel   128

Claude Le Jeune   129

Ludwig Senfl   130

Hans Leo Hassler   131

  Lied   133

Cristóbal de Morales 134

Antonio de Cabezón 136

  Villancico 138

Francisco Guerrero 139

Adriaan Willaert 139

Nicolas Gombert 140

Jacobus Clemens 141

Jan Pieterszoon Sweelinck 141

Conclusion 144

Glossary 145

Bibliography 147

Index 149

INTRODUCTION

The Renaissance was a period of expanding knowledge. Alongside a resurgence of interest in Classical learning, new ideas regarding science, religion, and the arts flourished and spread across Europe. Humanism, with its focus on human interests and values, steered prevailing thought toward nature, the individual, and the empirical. Renaissance musicians developed a variety of musical forms, respecting traditional modes of expression even as they expanded upon them. As this book details, the musicians of the period reflected to some degree the rapidly changing world around them.

Western music was influenced by that of the eastern Mediterranean in a number of ways, including the widespread adoption of the diatonic (seven-note) scale, which replaced the prevailing church modes commonly used until then, and the use of metre as a means of dividing compositions into equal portions of time. These are basic structural elements of classical composition.

The Christian Church was a vehicle of both musical evolution and dispersion. While there were many regional styles of chant, or unison songs, sung throughout Europe as part of the traditional Western church mass, Gregorian chant was the standard. Originating in Rome under Pope Gregory I in the late 6th century, this style of unison liturgical music was adopted across Europe over the next several hundred years, and then modified by the addition

Hand-coloured illustration from an early 16th-century edition of
Margarita philosophica *by German encyclopedist Gregor Reisch.*
Science & Society Picture Library/Getty Images

of melodic lines. This polyphony, which was both simultaneous and contrapuntal, was documented in the work of 11th-century monk and musical theorist Guido d'Arezzo.

In the 12th century, the main thrust of musical innovation shifted from Rome to Paris. At such places as Notre-Dame cathedral, music featuring multiple melodies that wove through or played against the plainsong melody was composed for liturgical, and later secular, use. Reflecting on the musical directions of his time, 14th-century French composer Philippe de Vitry wrote about the use of metre and harmony in his work *Ars Nova*; the label *Ars Antiqua* ("Ancient Art") came to apply to the music of the 13th century that had foreshadowed the changes to come.

From roughly the 15th century forward, royal interests shaped the evolution of music in more or less equal proportion to those of the Roman Catholic Church. The crème de la crème of European musicians were drawn to Burgundian courts (in what is now eastern France and portions of the Low Countries), attracted by the wealth of the French aristocracy and the promise of finding work in both the secular and religious realms. Early improvisational forms can be seen in compositions of this time, with melodies centred in the top voices and lower parts played by instruments. Some nobles became traveling musicians themselves, composing and performing songs in courts across France and Italy, calling themselves troubadours. These collections of composers and performers spread innovative ideas, including four-part harmony and chord progression, throughout Europe. Still, liturgical music remained in demand, and it evolved as well.

The secularization of music encouraged the development of new vocal styles. The reinvented madrigals of

16th century Italy evolved into dramatic, five- or even six-part harmonic pieces featuring complex texts and counterpoint (independent melodies that complemented and enriched the standard melody), while simpler songs, called *canzonettas* and *ballettos*, emerged as a response to the madrigal's complexity. The madrigal's French counterpart was known as the chanson. Composers in Elizabethan England adopted Italian madrigals, as well as *ballettos* and *canzonettas*, and made them their own, while also championing the popular ayre that sprang up in both countries. Germany was home to the lied, a secular song performed using straightforward chord progressions. Neither the lied nor the Spanish *villancico* of the Iberian Peninsula could match the madrigal in its stylistic importance.

Until the 16th century, music had been primarily vocal, with instruments serving primarily to double voices or accompany dancers. By the late 1500s, pieces written specifically for instruments exploded in popularity. They included traditional dance forms, such as the pavane and courante, as well as preludes (particularly for the organ), and fugue-like forms in which instrument voices imitated a melodic line, such as the *ricercari* and *canzoni*. No longer relegated to the role of mere accompaniment, instrumentalists began to showcase their own technical skills.

The lute in particular enjoyed mass popularity. Its strings, which varied in number before settling on six in the 16th century, were plucked with the fingers. The sound carried through the sound hole, reverberating in the instrument's hollow, pear-shaped body. Modified tunings produced a large assortment of variations on the lute.

Keyboard instruments also were favoured during the Renaissance. Among these was the pipe organ—a staple in churches, even to this day. Styles of organs varied by region, resulting in great variations in number of stops (pipes) and manual controls, but chromatic keyboards became standard as early as the 14th century. Also widespread at this time were stringed keyboards, including the clavichord and the harpsichord. The clavichord, designed for smaller venues than were organs, allowed the player to control dynamics solely through keystrokes. This typically rectangular instrument featured a keyboard on the left, and strings to the right, and had a range of three and a half to five octaves. The harpsichord outwardly resembles a modern piano, despite the frequent presence of two or more sets of strings. Unlike the clavichord and piano, which have hammered strings, the harpsichord makes music via strings that are plucked by a mechanism called a jack. Regional variations on the harpsichord were seen beginning in the 16th century. Smaller versions were called spinets, a name that now refers to one type of small upright piano. The virginal is a type of harpsichord in which the single set of strings runs nearly parallel to the keyboard, rather than in the perpendicular arrangement of other harpsichords.

Until the Renaissance, wind instruments had played a relatively limited musical role. With the development of polyphony and the increase in instrumental ensembles came the necessity for a range of instrumental voices. The result of this evolution in composition was a variety of instrument sizes. Renaissance wind instruments included recorders and cornets and such colourfully named devices as the shawm, sackbut, crumhorn, and hoboy (oboe).

The craftsmen who made and refined these instruments were responding to the needs of the composers of the Renaissance. The early composers of the period were pioneers of a rich, layered sound previously unknown. Described as graceful and expressive, compositions from a group of composers of what has become known as the

Franco-Flemish school marked a transition from the monophonic chants and diatonic pieces of the Middle Ages. Patronage of these men was provided by the church, nobility, or both at different points in their lives. Thus, nearly all wrote both religious and secular music.

Renaissance composers were an impressive lot. Hailing from various areas of Europe, each contributed to the evolution of musical styles and instrumentation. Some were employed by kings, such as Jean de Ockeghem, composer to three kings of France. Several began their musical careers as performers, such as Josquin de Prez, a singer whose mastery of composition was praised by German theologian and religious reformer Martin Luther. Attached, as they often were, by common service to an aristocrat, many early Renaissance composers often kept company with one another, as well as with poets and painters employed by the same court. The comingling of artistic sensibilities frequently yielded rich results. Regarded as a harmonic innovator, Englishman John Dunstable exerted great influence on composers of the Franco-Flemish school. Binchois used the poetry of Charles, duc d'Orleans, and Christine de Pisan for his texts, and was a contemporary of both the French composer Guillaume Dufay and the Flemish painter Jan van Eyck in the court of Philip the Good.

One might assume that, because of its geographic connection to the papacy in Rome, Italian music of the Renaissance would be predominantly sacred. However, as throughout Western Europe, both religious and secular works were produced by Italian composers of the time. Among those who were known for their madrigals was Jacques Arcadelt, a Flemish composer working in Italy, who set the poetry of the great Renaissance humanist Petrarch to music. The madrigals of Luca Marenzio are prized for their ability to reflect the mood of their texts, employing chromatics and unresolved dissonance to great effect.

Another composer of madrigals, Carlo Gesualdo, had an intriguing personal life that threatened to overshadow his music. A prince who murdered his first wife and her lover, and whose second wife claimed that his lovers performed witchcraft on him, Gesualdo created work that has been described as "unusual and experimental."

As a choirboy with an exceptionally fine voice, the Flemish composer Orlando di Lasso was "kidnapped" and pressed into service for various choirs on three separate occasions. In adulthood, Lasso worked for several nobles, traveling with them before settling in Germany. While adept at writing secular music in the French, German, and Italian styles, Lasso was particularly noted for his sacred works. His compositions helped earn him the rank of noble, granted by the Emperor Maximilian, and a high pontifical honour from Pope Gregory XIII.

While the likes of Gesualdo and Lasso drew inspiration from the unconventional circumstances of their own lives, another composer of this period, Claudio Monteverdi, mostly left drama at the theatre door, as it were. A composer who occasionally wrote for the dramatic stage, Monteverdi became a master of the operatic score. His attempts to match the music to the emotions being exhibited onstage via tempo and dissonance, as well as his experimentation with musical forms such as the recitative (music free of rhythm that imitates natural speech), shaped the then-burgeoning art of opera. His influence is still felt today.

Patronage was extremely important to Renaissance musicians and composers. Both secular and religious works were often dedicated to the noblemen or church elders whose financing made their completion possible.

However, some composers succeeded despite lacking in privilege. Although he held nonmusical positions under two bishops in his native France, Clément Janequin never received patronage from anyone in the church, nor from anyone at court. Despite this lack of support, Janequin published a number of works; he is particularly known for his chansons. Swiss composer Ludwig Senfl endured a period of what essentially amounted to unemployment after the death of his patron, the Holy Roman Emperor Maximilian I, but he was able to regain his status several years later.

Religious affiliation also was a crucial element in the lives of many of these men. The division between Catholics and Protestants during the later Renaissance set the stage for a period of great musical productivity in England. The composer Christopher Tye was greatly influential in creating the style of music adopted by the Reformed church, adhering to the dictates of King Edward VI, who decreed that choirs sing in English and use one note per syllable. Upon Tye's death, Thomas Tallis took up the mantle of leadership through the creation of settings for the new liturgy in the Church of England. The settings were analogous to parts of the Latin mass in the Roman Catholic Church. Tallis's pupil, William Byrd, was a Catholic, yet he wrote for both churches, as the political climate allowed. Composer and musician John Dowland was convinced that his conversion to Catholicism was responsible for his loss of a post as court lutenist, resulting in years of self-exile from England. Dowland's time abroad proved useful as he was able to incorporate musical styles and innovations gleaned from across the Continent into his own work, which included 90 pieces for solo lute.

In addition to Dowland, there are plenty of other musicians whose work benefited from the mingling of ideas across countries and regions. Philippe de Monte's madrigals were influenced by his travels and periods of residence in Italy, England, Spain, and other locations across Europe. Evidence of exposure to other musical cultures can be found as well in the compositions of Hans Leo Hassler, a German composer whose works show Italian characteristics. Innovations made by musicians of the age formed a bridge leading from medieval chants and common songs to the great modern classical composers. It is hard to imagine what modern music would be like without these crucial transitions. Hence, the study of Renaissance musicians and their work is crucial toward gaining a clear understanding of the evolution of Western music.

Chapter 1

THE TRANSITION TO THE RENAISSANCE

When the musical culture of the eastern Mediterranean was transplanted into the western Mediterranean by the returning Roman legions, it was inevitably modified by local tastes and traditions. In most cases, the practices that resulted from these intersections of styles were more limited than their models. The diatonic (seven-note) scale, for example, became the standard, displacing the standard structures of the Grecian system. Of particular consequence was the new concept of metre as a series of equal durations, with emphasis being determined by accent (stress) rather than by duration.

An inventory of the musical heritage transplanted from the ancient East (particularly Greece) to Rome reveals the rich treasure inherited: an acoustical theory that accounted for the identification and classification of tones; a concept of tonal organization resulting in the system of modes; principles of rhythmic organization; basic principles of instrument construction; a system of notation that conveyed all necessary indications of pitch and duration; and a large repertory of melodies to serve as models for further composition.

With the decline of the Roman Empire, the institution destined to perpetuate and expand the musical heritage of antiquity was the Christian Church, but it was not a unified process. Many of the cultural centres of the Western church developed distinctive characteristics while sharing the common heritage of the Hebrew liturgy and Greek culture. In Milan, for example, metrical hymnody, as distinguished from the earlier practice of unmetred psalmody, was cultivated, particularly under the influence of the 4th-century Bishop Ambrose, who first attempted to codify the growing repertory of chants. This body of Milanese church music used to accompany the Latin mass and canonical hours of the Ambrosian rite came to be called Ambrosian chant. Elsewhere, as in Spain (Mozarabic chant) and France (Gallican style), other styles and repertories prevailed.

But the mainstream of church music was the type of chant practiced in Rome. Beginning in the late 6th century,

Pope Gregory I, depicted by the artist as teaching young choristers to sing the chant that is named for him. Gregorian chant was the leading form of church music for ages. Hulton Archive/Getty Images

according to tradition, with Pope Gregory I, the vast number of traditional melodies that became the foundation for the later development of Western art music were codified and organized. A systematic organization of tonal materials also was gradually accomplished, resulting in the eight church modes. Each melody was assigned a specific function in the services of the liturgical year—some for the mass and some for the divine offices such as Matins (morning prayer), Vespers (evening prayer), and Compline (service before retiring for the day).

After a period of assimilation, the Gregorian chant repertory began a process of expansion in the 9th century, when the practice of troping originated. A trope is either a text or a melodic section added to a preexisting melody or a combination of text and music incorporated into existing liturgical music. It is not surprising that church musicians, after years of singing traditional chants, should want to express themselves by adding words to vocalized melodies. Perhaps the motive was more functional: the added syllables would make the long textless passages easier to remember. Tuotilo (died 915), a monk of St. Gall in Switzerland, is credited with the invention of tropes. Notker Balbulus (died 912) is notable for his association with the sequence, a long hymn that originated as a trope added to the final syllable of the Alleluia of the mass.

DEVELOPMENT OF POLYPHONY

At the same time that the Gregorian repertory was being expanded by the interpolation of tropes and sequences, it was being further enriched by a revolutionary concept destined to give a new direction to the art of sound for hundreds of years. This concept was polyphony, or the simultaneous sounding of two or more melodic lines. Lack of definite knowledge regarding the origins of this musical practice, which emerged gradually during the Dark Ages, has brought forward several plausible theories. One is that polyphony resulted from singers with different natural vocal ranges singing at their most comfortable pitch levels. Other theories hold that it was a practice of organists adopted by singers, or it came about when the repetition of a melody at a different pitch level was sung simultaneously with the original statement of the melody.

Whatever motivated this dramatic departure from traditional monophony (music consisting of a single voice part), it was an established practice when it was described in *Musica enchiriadis* (c. 900), a manual for singers and one of the major musical documents of the Middle Ages. To a given plainsong, or *vox principalis*, a second voice (*vox organalis*) could be added at the interval (distance between notes) of a fourth or fifth (four or five steps) below. Music so performed was known as organum. While it may be assumed that the first attempts at polyphony involved only parallel motion at a set interval, the *Musica enchiriadis* describes and gives examples of two-part singing in similar (but not exactly parallel) and contrary movement—evidence that a considerable process of evolution had already taken place.

The next major source of information was the *Micrologus*, written in the early 11th century by the Italian monk and musical theorist Guido d'Arezzo. This work documented principles that were crucial to the further development of polyphony. Rhythmic independence was added to melodic independence, and the added voice might sing two or more tones to one in the original plainsong. During the half century after Guido's death, developments came more rapidly as the plainsong chant became the lower rather than the upper voice. After the emancipation of the organal part, *vox organalis*, its ultimate freedom was reached in the organums of the

GUIDO D'AREZZO

The medieval music theorist Guido d'Arezzo established principles that served as a foundation for modern Western musical notation. He was born probably in Arezzo about 990. Educated at the Benedictine abbey at Pomposa, Guido evidently made use of the music treatise of Odo of Saint-Maur-des-Fossés and apparently developed his principles of staff notation there. He left Pomposa in about 1025 because his fellow monks resisted his musical innovations, and he was appointed by Theobald, bishop of Arezzo, as a teacher in the cathedral school and commissioned to write the *Micrologus de disciplina artis musicae*. The bishop also arranged for Guido to give (c. 1028) to Pope John XIX an antiphonary he had begun in Pomposa.

Guido seems to have gone to the Camaldolese monastery at Avellana in 1029, and his fame developed from there. Many of the 11th-century manuscripts notated in the new manner came from Camaldolese houses.

The fundamentals of the new method consisted in the construction by thirds of a system of four lines, or staff, and the use of letters as clefs. The red F-line and the yellow C-line were already in use, but Guido added a black line between the F and the C and another black line above the C. The neumes (predecessors to modern musical notes) could now be placed on the lines and spaces between and a definite pitch relationship established. No longer was it necessary to learn melodies by rote, and Guido declared that his system reduced the 10 years normally required to become an ecclesiastical singer to a year.

Guido was also developing the technique of solmization—using syllables to denote the tones of a musical scale—described in his *Epistola de ignoto cantu*. There is no evidence that the Guidonian hand, a mnemonic device associated with his name and widely used in the Middle Ages, had any connection with Guido d'Arezzo.

Guido is also credited with the composition of a hymn to St. John the Baptist, *Ut queant laxis*, in which the first syllable of each line falls on a different tone of the hexachord (the first six tones of the major scale). These syllables, *ut*, *re*, *mi*, *fa*, *sol*, and *la*, are used in Latin countries as the names of the notes from *c* to *a* (*ut* was eventually replaced by *do*). His device was of immense practical value in teaching sight-reading of music and in learning melodies. Singers associated the syllables with certain intervals; *mi* to *fa*, in particular, always represented a half step.

Before Guido, an alphabetical notation using the letters from *a* to *p* was used in France as early as 996. Guido's system used a series of capital letters, small letters, and double small letters from *a* to *g*. Guido's system also came to be associated with the teaching of the gamut—the whole hexachord range (the range of notes available to the singer).

monastery of Saint-Martial in Limoges, France, where the plainsong part was reduced to the role of sustaining each tone while the organal part indulged in free melismata (groups of notes sung to a single syllable), either improvised or composed. This new style was called *organum purum*.

THE NOTRE-DAME SCHOOL

Early in the 12th century the centre of musical activity shifted to the church of Notre-Dame in Paris, where the French composer Léonin recorded in the *Magnus Liber Organi* ("Great Book of Organum") a collection of two-part organums for the entire church year. A generation later his successor, Pérotin, edited and revised the *Magnus Liber*, incorporating the rhythmic patterns already well-known

Ornately decorated page of church music from the Notre-Dame school, featuring Latin text. Universal Images Group/Getty Images

in secular music and adding more than one part to the cantus firmus (the "given" or preexisting plainsong melody). When metre was applied to the original plainsong as well as to the *vox organalis*, the resulting form was called a clausula. Then, when words were provided for the added part or parts, a clausula became a motet. At first the words given to the motet were a commentary in Latin on the text of the original plainsong tenor (the voice part "holding" the cantus firmus; from Latin *tenere*, "to hold"). Later in the 13th century the added words were in French and secular in nature.

Finally, each added part was given its own text, resulting in the classic Paris motet: a three-part composition consisting of a portion of plainchant (tenor) overlaid with two faster moving parts, each with its own secular text in French. At the same time another polyphonic form, the conductus, was flourishing. It differed from a motet in that its basic part was not plainsong and that all parts sang the same Latin text in note-against-note style. The conductus gradually disappeared with the rise of the motet, which apparently served both liturgical and secular functions.

ARS NOVA

When the influential treatise *Ars Nova* ("New Art") by the composer Philippe de Vitry appeared early in the 14th century, the preceding epoch acquired its designation of Ars Antiqua ("Old Art"), for it was only in retrospect that the rapid developments of the century and a half from c. 1150 to c. 1300 could appear as antiquated. De Vitry recorded the innovations of his day, particularly in the areas of metre and harmony. While 13th-century music had been organized around the triple "modal" rhythms derived from secular music and a harmonic vocabulary based on "perfect" consonances (unison, fourth, fifth, octave), the

ARS ANTIQUA

The period of musical activity in 13th-century France, characterized by increasingly sophisticated counterpoint (the art of combining simultaneous voice parts), was known as Ars Antiqua. It culminated in the innovations of the 14th-century Ars Nova. The term itself originated, in fact, with the Ars Nova theorists, some of whom spoke of the "Ancient Art" with praise, others with contempt. All of them, however, agreed upon a marked difference between the two styles, a difference rooted primarily in the profound rhythmic innovations of the Ars Nova. Those theorists limited the Ars Antiqua to the latter part of the 13th century, while modern music historians have broadened the term to encompass the entire century.

The authorship of most of the music of the Ars Antiqua is anonymous. Nevertheless, three important figures emerge from the general obscurity: Pérotin (flourished late 12th century), who succeeded the famed Léonin at the Cathedral of Notre-Dame in Paris and who composed the earliest known music for four voices; Franco of Cologne (flourished mid-13th century), a theorist, whose *Ars cantus mensurabilis* ("The Art of Measured Song") served to organize and codify the newly formed mensural system (a more precise system of rhythmic notation, the direct ancestor of modern notation); and Pierre de la Croix (flourished last half of 13th century), whose works anticipate the Ars Nova style by virtue of their rhythmic fluency.

The most important form to originate in the Ars Antiqua is the motet, which retained its popularity for centuries. The essence of this form is its simultaneous presentation of more than one text. It seems to have begun with the addition of a new text to the upper voice(s) of a sacred polyphonic composition, the slower moving lower voice retaining its original sacred text. The next text—in Latin, like the original text—at first complemented or amplified the meaning of the original words. Later, the language of the added text changed to French while the sentiments became more worldly, resulting in compositions in which the sacred Latin text of the lower voice is accompanied by one or more secular French texts in the upper voice(s).

New Art of the 14th century used duple as well as triple divisions of the basic pulse and brought about a taste for harmonious intervals of thirds and sixths.

The musical centre of 14th-century Italy was Florence, where a blind organist, Francisco Landini, and his predecessors and contemporaries Giovanni da Cascia, Jacopo da Bologna, and Lorenzo and Ghirardello da Firenze were the leading composers of several new forms: madrigals (contrapuntal compositions for several voices), *ballata*s (similar to the French *virelai*), and *caccia*s (three-voice songs using melodic imitation).

MONOPHONIC SECULAR SONG

Secular music undoubtedly flourished during the early Middle Ages, but, aside from sporadic references, the earliest accounts of such music in the Western world described the music of the goliards. These people were itinerant minor clerics and students who, from the 7th century on, roamed the land singing and playing topical songs dealing with love, war, famine, and other issues of the day. The emergence in France of a fully developed secular-musical tradition about the beginning of the 12th century is evidence that the art had been evolving continuously before that time.

Image of a troubadour performing outside a castle wall. © Pantheon/
SuperStock

Partially motivated by the attitude of chivalry engendered by the Crusades, a new lifestyle began among the nobility of southern France. Calling themselves troubadours, they circulated among the leading courts of the region, devoting themselves to writing and singing poetry in the vernacular. The troubadour movement flourished in Provence during the 12th and 13th centuries. About the middle of the 12th century, noblemen of northern France, most notably Adam de La Halle, took up the pastime, calling themselves trouvères.

In Germany a similar group known as minnesingers, represented by Walther von der Vogelweide, began their activities about 1150 and continued for almost a century after their French counterparts had ceased composing. Late in the 13th century the burgher class in Germany began imitating the aristocratic minnesingers. Calling themselves Meistersingers, they flourished for more than 500 years, organizing themselves into fraternities and following strict rules of poetry, music, and performance. The most famous of them, Hans Sachs, was immortalized in the 19th century in Richard Wagner's opera *Die Meistersinger von Nürnberg*.

Relatively little is known of similar secular-musical activities in Italy, Spain, and England. Closely associated with the entertainments of the aristocratic dilettantes were the professional musicians of the peasant class called jongleurs and minstrels in France, *Gaukler* in Germany, and scops and gleemen in England.

The musical style that had been established by the troubadours—which was monophonic, of limited range, and sectional in structure—was adopted by each of the succeeding groups. Of particular significance in view of its influence on polyphonic music was the metric system, which is based on six rhythmic modes. Supposedly derived from Greek poetic metres such as trochaic (long–short) and iambic (short–long), these modes brought about a prevailing triple metre in French music, while German poetry produced duple as well as triple metre. A great variety of formal patterns evolved, in which musical structure and poetic structure were closely related. The most characteristic was the ballade, which was called *Bar* form in Germany, with an AAB structure.

This type, along with the rondeau (song for solo voice with choral refrain) and the similar *virelai* (an analogue of the Italian *ballata*), was destined to become a favoured form employed by composers of polyphony such as Guillaume de Machaut, the universally acknowledged master of French music of the Ars Nova period. Machaut also continued the composition of motets, organizing them around recurrent rhythmic patterns (isorhythm), a major structural technique of the age. The beginnings of an independent instrumental repertory during the 13th century are represented by the *estampie*, a monophonic dance form almost identical in style to the vocal secular music.

THE EARLY RENAISSANCE

The term *Renaissance*, in spite of its various connotations, is difficult to apply to music. Borrowed from the visual arts and literature, the term is meaningful primarily as a chronological designation. Some historians date the beginning of the musical Renaissance at about 1400, some with the rise of imitative counterpoint, about 1450. Others relate it to the musical association with humanistic poetry at the beginning of the 16th century, and still others reserve the term for the conscious attempt to recreate and imitate supposedly classical models that took place about 1600.

THE COURT OF BURGUNDY

No one line of demarcation is completely satisfactory, but, adhering to commonly accepted usage, one may conveniently accept as the beginning of the musical Renaissance the flourishing and secularization of music at the beginning of the 15th century, particularly at the court of Burgundy. Certainly many manifestations of a cultural renaissance were evident at the time: interest in preserving artifacts and literature of classical antiquity, the waning authority and influence of the church, the waxing humanism, the burgeoning of urban centres and universities, and the growing economic affluence of the states of western Europe.

As one manifestation of their cultivation of elegant living, the aristocracy of both church and state vied with one another in maintaining resident musicians who could serve both chapel and banqueting hall. The frequent interchange of these musicians accounts for the rapid dissemination of new musical techniques and tastes. Partly because of economic advantages, Burgundy and its capital, Dijon, became the centre of European activity in music as well as the intellectual and artistic focus of northern Europe during the first half of the 15th century. Comprising most of eastern France and the Low Countries, the courts of Philip the Good and Charles the Bold attracted the leading musicians of western Europe. Prime among them was Guillaume Dufay, who had spent some time in Rome and Florence before settling in Cambrai about 1440. An important contemporary of Dufay was Binchois (Gilles de Binche), who served at Dijon from about 1430 until 1460. The alliance of Burgundy with England accounted for the presence on the Continent of the English composer John Dunstable, who had a profound influence on Dufay. While the contributions of the English to the mainstream of Continental music are sparsely documented, the differences in style between Dufay and his predecessor Machaut are partially accounted for by the new techniques and, especially, the richer harmonies adopted by the Burgundian composers from their English allies.

NEW RELIGIOUS MUSICAL FORMS

The social circumstances of the age determined that composers would devote their efforts to the mass, the motet, and the chanson (secular French song). During the first half of the 15th century, the mass became established as a unified polyphonic setting of the five main parts of the Ordinary of the mass (Kyrie, Gloria, Credo, Sanctus, Agnus Dei), with each movement based on either the relevant portion of plainsong or, reflecting the dawning Renaissance, a secular song such as the popular "L'Homme armé" ("The Armed Man") and "Se la face ay pale." Still reflecting medieval practices, the preexisting melody (or cantus firmus) was usually in the tenor (or lowest) part and in long, sustained tones, while the upper parts provided free elaboration.

Dufay's nine complete settings of the mass, compared with Machaut's single setting, give a clear indication of the growing importance of the mass as a musical form. The motet became simply a setting of a Latin text from Scriptures or the liturgy in the prevailing polyphonic style of the time. It was no longer necessarily anchored to a plainsong tenor. The composer could give free reign to his invention, although some did, of course, resort to older techniques.

SECULAR MUSIC

It was in secular music that giant strides took place. While they also continued the tradition of rondeaux, *virelais*, and ballades, Dufay and his contemporaries added free forms divorced from these ordered patterns of the Ars Antiqua and Ars Nova periods.

Among the distinctive features of Burgundian musical style was the prevailing three-part texture, with melodic and rhythmic interest centred in the top part. Because it was so typical of secular songs, this texture is commonly referred to as "ballade style" whether it appears in sacred or secular music. Its possible stylistic implication is that a solo voice sang the upper melody, accompanied by instruments playing the lower parts, although no documents remain to establish exactly how the music was performed. There was probably no standard performing medium: all parts may have been sung; some or all may have been doubled by instruments; or there may have been one vocal part supported by instrumental accompaniment.

THE FRANCO-FLEMISH SCHOOL

A watershed in the history of music occurred about the middle of the 15th century. The fall of Constantinople (now Istanbul) in 1453 and the end of the Hundred Years' War at about the same time increased commerce from the East and affluence in the West. Most significant musically was the pervasive influence of musicians from the Low Countries, whose domination of the musical scene during the last half of the 15th century is reflected in the period designations the Netherlands school and the Franco-Flemish (or Franco-Netherlandish) school. These musicians travelled and resided throughout Europe in response to their great demand at princely courts, including those of the Medici family in Florence and the Sforzas in Milan. Further dissemination of knowledge resulted from the invention and development of printing.

The leading composers, whose patrons were now members of the civil aristocracy as well as princes of the church, were Jean de Ockeghem, Jakob Obrecht, and, especially, Josquin des Prez. De Ockeghem, born and trained in Flanders, spent most of his life in the service of the kings of France and was recognized by his contemporaries as the "Prince of Music." Obrecht remained near his birthplace in the Netherlands, going occasionally to Italy in the retinue of Duke Ercole I of Ferrara. More typical of the peripatetic Netherlanders was the career of Josquin, the most influential composer of the period. After training at St. Quentin, he served the Sforza family in Milan, the papal choir in Rome, Ercole I, and King Louis XII of France before returning to his native Flanders in 1516. These three composers and several contemporaries hastened the development of the musical techniques that became the basis of 16th-century practice and influenced succeeding developments.

Rather than the three parts typical of most Burgundian music, four parts became standard for vocal polyphony in the late 15th century. The fourth part was added below the tenor, increasing the total range and resulting in greater breadth of sound. The presence of the four parts also allowed for contrasts of texture such as the "duet style" so characteristic of Josquin, when the two upper parts might sing a passage alone and be echoed by the two lower parts alone. The emergence of the technique of imitation (one voice repeating recognizably a figure heard first in another voice) as the chief form-generating principle brought about more equality of parts. At the same time "familiar style," in which all parts move together in chords, provided a means of textural contrast. The great variety of rhythmic techniques that evolved during the 14th and early 15th centuries made possible a wide range of expression—from quiet tranquillity for sacred music to lively and spirited secular music. Knowledge of the musical practices comes not only from the thousands of surviving compositions but from informative treatises such as the 12 by the composer Johannes Tinctoris (1436–1511), one of which, *Terminorum musicae diffinitorium* (c. 1475), is the earliest printed dictionary of musical terms.

INSTRUMENTAL MUSIC

At the same time, an independent instrumental idiom was evolving. While instruments had been in common usage throughout the Middle Ages, their function was primarily to double or to substitute for voices in vocal polyphonic music or to provide music for dancing. Techniques unsuitable for voices were doubtless part of an instrumentalist's musical vocabulary, but most such music was improvised rather than being written. Although there are a few sources of instrumental music dating from the 13th and 14th centuries, the earliest relatively extensive documentation comes from the 15th century, particularly from German sources, such as the *Buxheimer Orgelbuch* and Conrad Paumann's *Fundamentum organisandi* (*Fundamentals of Organ Playing*). The compositions in both collections are of two basic types, arrangements of vocal works and keyboard pieces entitled *Praeambulum* (*Prelude*).

During the course of the 16th century, instrumental music burgeoned rapidly, along with the continually developing idiomatically instrumental techniques, such as strongly accented rhythms, rapid repeated tones and figures, angular melodic lines involving wide intervallic skips, wide ranges, long, sustained tones and phrases, and much melodic ornamentation.

MUSICAL FORMS

Dance forms, a continuation of a tradition unbroken since the beginnings of recorded music history, were most characteristically composed in pairs, although single dances as well as embryonic suites of three or more dances appeared. The pairs usually consisted of pieces in contrasting tempo and metre that often were unified by sharing a common melody. Common dance pairs included the pavane and galliard, the allemande and courante, and the basse danse and tourdion.

Preludes continued as a major form of organ music and were joined by the fantasia, the *intonazione*, and the toccata in a category frequently referred to as "free forms" because of the inconsistency and unpredictability of their structure and musical content—sections in imitative counterpoint, sections of sustained chords, sections in virtuoso figuration. If a distinction must be made, it might be said in very general terms that the fantasia tended to be more contrapuntal while the toccata (or "touch piece") featured passages designed to demonstrate the performer's agility, although the designations were freely interchangeable. To the same category belong the descriptive pieces such as *The King's Hunt*, which featured naive musical representations of natural sounds.

The ricercar and the canzona, generally referred to as fugal forms because of their relationship to the principle of the fugue (that of melodic imitation), arose out of the growing understanding of and dependence on imitation as a unifying structural technique. Although these designations were applied to a great variety of pieces—some identical in style to the fantasia or prelude—the classic ricercar of the 16th century was virtually an instrumental motet, slow and churchlike in character and consisting

TOCCATA

The toccata, a musical form for keyboard instruments, is written in a free style characterized by full chords, rapid runs, high harmonies, and other virtuoso elements designed to show off the performer's "touch." The earliest use of the term (about 1536) was associated with solo lute music of an improvisatory character.

In the late 16th century in Venice such composers as Giovanni Gabrieli and Claudio Merulo wrote organ toccatas (many with such titles as *Fantasia* and *Intonazione*), often achieving a majestic virtuosity by means of florid scale passages, embellishments, unsteady rhythms and harmonies, changes of mood, and freedom of tempo. Merulo initiated the later common practice of alternating fugal sections (using melodic imitation) with rapid toccata passages. In Rome, Girolamo Frescobaldi (d. 1643) composed toccatas that consisted of highly improvisatory sections loosely strung together, marked by sudden changes in harmonies and figuration. They were intended to be played with a free tempo and could be performed in their entirety or in one or more sections. Frescobaldi's German pupil Johann Jakob Froberger was an important transmitter of the style to Germany. Like his teacher, Froberger delighted in the use of chromatic harmonies (using notes foreign to the mode of the piece); and, like Merulo, he characteristically placed a contrasting fugal section between introductory and closing passages in toccata style.

The juxtaposition of improvisatory and fugal passages — which appealed to the Baroque fascination with the union of opposites — became a prominent feature of the toccatas of the organist-composers of north Germany, culminating in the works of Dietrich Buxtehude and, later, J.S. Bach.

of a number of sections, each utilizing imitation. The canzona followed the same structural principle but was a lively counterpart to the chanson, with the sections sometimes in contrasting tempo and metre. Cantus firmus compositions were based upon preexisting melody. During the 16th century most were designed for liturgical usage but were based upon both secular melodies and plainsong. In most cases the cantus firmus was sounded in

A scene featuring monks singing and playing the organ. In the 16th century, choir members and the organ often alternated lines of melody when performing liturgical (church) music. Danita Delimont/Gallo Images/Getty Images

long, sustained tones while the other part or parts added decorative contrapuntal lines. The organ mass, in which the choir and the organ alternated lines of the liturgical text, was a popular practice.

Variations also often used a preexisting melody but differed from cantus firmus compositions in that the melody was much shorter and was repeated a number of times, each time with different accompanying parts. The two basic types during the Renaissance were the plain, or melodic, variations and the ground. In the former, the chosen melody usually appeared in the top part and was varied in each repetition with ornamentation and melodic figuration or with changing accompaniments. The ground, or ground bass, was a simple melodic pattern sounded in the lowest part, which served as a foundation for imaginative figuration in the upper parts.

SOLO AND ENSEMBLE INSTRUMENTS

The four major vehicles for instrumental music of the period were the lute, the organ, stringed keyboard instruments, and instrumental ensembles. Most popular by far was the lute, which could produce the major elements of instrumental style except for long, sustained tones. Noteworthy composers of lute music included Luis Milán in Spain, Arnold Schlick in Germany, and John Dowland in England. The organ, because of its close association with liturgical music, continued to be an important instrument, and its literature includes all of the formal types except dances. Among the leading organ composers were the Germans Paumann, Schlick, and Paul Hofhaimer, the Italians Claudio Merulo and Andrea and Giovanni Gabrieli, the Spaniard Antonio de Cabezón, and the Englishman John Bull.

Angel playing a lute, from "Presentation in the Temple," painted altarpiece by Vittore Carpaccio, 1510; in the Accademia, Venice. SCALA/ Art Resource, New York

The two basic classes of stringed keyboard instruments were the harpsichord (virginals, spinet, clavecin, clavicembalo), with quill-plucked strings, and the clavichord, with strings struck by thin metal tongues. Keyboard instruments were highly capable of idiomatically instrumental effects and flourished, particularly in England, from the last half of the 16th century onward, thanks to the composers William Byrd, John Bull, and Orlando Gibbons.

Instrumental ensembles of the Renaissance were not standardized, although consorts (groups) of viols, of woodwind instruments such as recorders and shawms (loud oboes), or of brass-family instruments such as the cornet and sackbut (early trombone) were common. More common, however, were mixed consorts of various types of instruments, depending on the players available. All types of instrumental forms were performed by ensembles except for the prelude and the toccata, which were essentially keyboard works. Representative composers included the Gabrielis and Gibbons.

RENAISSANCE VOCAL MUSIC

At the beginning of the 16th century the style of vocal music was generally uniform because of the pervading influence of Netherlanders during the preceding half century. That uniformity persisted well into the late Renaissance but was gradually superseded by emerging national differences, new forms, and the increasing importance of Italy as a musical centre during the last half of the 16th century.

The rapid accumulation of new musical techniques and resources produced a wide vocabulary of artistic expression, and the invention of music printing helped the rapid dispersal of new techniques. In an age in which music was an essential social grace, composers wrote more secular music, in which fewer technical restrictions were in force and experimentation and novelty were applauded. Advances were particularly apparent in venturesome harmonies as chromaticism (the use of notes not belonging to the mode of the composition) sounded the death knell of the modal system.

Liturgical practice dictated that the mass and the motet remain the chief forms of sacred vocal music. Compared with secular music, their style was conservative, but inevitably some of the newer secular techniques crept in and figured effectively in the music of the Counter-Reformation within the Roman Catholic Church.

Four distinct types of mass settings were established during the century. Two types were continuations of earlier practice: the tenor mass, in which the same cantus firmus served for all five portions of the Ordinary of the mass, and the plainsong mass, in which the cantus firmus (usually a corresponding section of plainsong) differed for each portion. Reflecting the more liberal attitudes of the Renaissance were the free mass, with no borrowed materials, and the parody mass, in which the entire polyphonic web was freely adapted from a motet or a secular composition. In all cases when a cantus firmus was used, the preexistent melody might appear in its original form or in paraphrased version, with tones added, omitted, or altered. As a result of the upheaval in the church caused by the Reformation, new forms derived from established models appeared in Protestant worship: the German Lutheran chorale (hymn tune, arranged from plainsong or a secular melody), the chorale motet, English anthems (Anglican form of motet) and services, and the psalm tunes in Calvinist areas.

ITALY

While not young in a chronological sense, the musical life of Italy was reborn at the beginning of the 16th century after a century of relative dormancy. The *frottola* remained the prevailing secular form in northern Italy for the first three decades of the century.

When the humanistic poets, seeking a more refined expression, and the Netherlanders and composers trained by them, applying a more sophisticated musical technique, turned their efforts to the *frottola*, the result was the madrigal. The name was borrowed from the 14th-century form, but there was no resemblance in poetic or musical structure. Compared to the *frottola*, the earliest Renaissance madrigals, dating from about 1530, were characterized by quiet and restrained expression. Usually written for three or four voices, they were mostly homophonic (melody supported by chords) with occasional bits of imitation. Among the early madrigal composers were several Flemish composers resident in Italy, among them Adriaan Willaert, Jacques Arcadelt, and Philippe Verdelot. About 1560 the normal number of parts increased to five or six, and the texture became more consistently polyphonic. At the same time, more attention was given to expressive settings of the text, notably in the madrigals of Cipriano de Rore, Philippe de Monte, and the Gabrielis. During the last two decades of the century and continuing until the middle of the 17th century, the musical style of the madrigal changed appreciably. The late madrigals were of a very dramatic nature, featuring colouristic effects, vivid word-painting, and extensive chromaticism. Their declamatory character dictated a return to a more homophonic style. Noteworthy among the many composers of the late madrigal were Luca Marenzio, Carlo Gesualdo, and Claudio Monteverdi.

During the course of the century simpler secular forms, such as the *villanella*, the *canzonetta*, and the *balletto*, appeared in Italy, largely as a reaction against the refinement, complication, and sophistication of the madrigal. They reverted to the chordal style of the *frottola*, often with intentionally parodistic lyrics. The *balletto* was particularly distinguished by a refrain of nonsense syllables such as "fa la la."

ENGLAND

Most of the Italian forms, along with their designations, were adopted by Elizabethan England during the last half of the 16th century. Most leading English composers, from William Byrd and Thomas Morley to John Wilbye, Thomas Weelkes, and Orlando Gibbons, contributed to the vast treasury of English secular music. Morley is particularly important as the editor of the most significant collection of English madrigals, the *Triumphes of Oriana*, published in 1603 and dedicated to Queen Elizabeth I (Oriana). These pieces correspond in style roughly to the middle-period Italian madrigal. English counterparts of the *canzonetta* and *balletto* were the canzonet and ballett. A late 16th-century innovation in both Italy and England was the ayre (air), a simple, chordal setting especially suitable for a solo voice with a lute or a consort of instruments playing the other parts. John Dowland and Thomas Campion were notable composers of ayres.

FRANCE

The French counterpart of Italian and English madrigals was the polyphonic chanson, a continuation of the chief medieval and early Renaissance form of secular music. Revitalized by composers such as Josquin, Clément Janequin, and Claudin de Sermisy, the chanson developed several distinctive features: a clearly delineated sectional structure with some repetition of sections, much vivid programmatic writing, and occasional use of irregular metric organization. The irregular metric structure, called *musique mesurée*, was used for maintaining faithfully the accentuation of the poetry and reflects the traditional primacy of textual over musical considerations in French music.

GERMANY AND OTHER AREAS OF EUROPE

The lied, or song, continued its 15th-century role as the chief secular form in Germanic areas, but it did not develop to the same extent as the madrigal and the chanson. Throughout the Renaissance it was relatively conservative in its adherence to the cantus firmus principle and its tendency toward chordal over contrapuntal texture. Following Heinrich Isaac in the 15th century, the major 16th-century lieder composers were Ludwig Senfl, Hans Leo Hassler, and Johann Hermann Schein. To all national schools of the 16th century must be added the name of the Flemish composer Orlando di Lasso, who wrote in French, Italian, or German, depending on his current employment. The Spanish *villancico* was a flourishing popular form, but there was no Iberian equivalent to the madrigal, the chanson, or the lied.

CHAPTER 2

RENAISSANCE MUSICAL INSTRUMENTS

Many of the instruments popular in medieval and Renaissance Europe came from Asia, having been transmitted through Byzantium, Spain, or eastern Europe. Perhaps the most notable development in western Europe was the practice, originating apparently in the 15th century, of building instruments in families, from the smallest to the largest size. A typical family was that of the shawms, which were powerful double-reed instruments. A distinction was made between *haut* (loud) and *bas* (soft) instruments, the former being suitable for performance out-of-doors and the latter for more intimate occasions. Hence, the shawm came to be known as the *hautbois* (loud wood), and this name was transferred to its more delicately toned descendant, the 17th-century oboe. By the beginning of the 17th century the German musical writer and composer Michael Praetorius, in his *Syntagma musicum* ("Musical Treatise"), was able to give a detailed account of families of instruments of all kinds—recorders, flutes, shawms, trombones, viols, and violins.

LUTE

One of the major instruments of the Renaissance was the lute, a plucked or bowed chordophone—one of a class of

Instruments in the shawm family, like the one pictured on the left (next to a smaller transverse Spanish clarinet, known as a pito), were made in a variety of sizes. Odile Noel/Redferns/Getty Images

musical instruments (also including harps, lyres, bows, and zithers) whose initial sound is produced by a stretched, vibrating string. A lute has strings parallel to its belly, or soundboard, that run along a distinct neck or pole. In this sense, instruments such as the Indian sitar are classified as lutes. The violin and the Indonesian *rebab* are bowed lutes, and the Japanese samisen and the Western guitar are plucked lutes.

In Europe, the term *lute* refers specifically to a plucked stringed musical instrument popular in the 16th and 17th centuries. The lute that was prominent in European popular art and music of the Renaissance and Baroque periods originated as the Arab *'ūd* (oud). This instrument was taken to Europe in the 13th century by way of Spain and by returning crusaders and is still played in Arab countries. Like the *'ūd*, the European lute has a deep, pear-shaped body, a neck with a bent-back pegbox, and strings hitched to a tension, or guitar-type, bridge glued to the instrument's belly. European lutes have a large, circular sound hole cut into the belly and ornamented with a perforated rose carved from the belly's wood.

The earliest European lutes followed the Arab instruments in having four strings plucked with a quill plectrum. By the mid-14th century the strings had become pairs, or courses. During the 15th century the plectrum was abandoned in favour of playing with the fingers, movable gut frets were added to the fingerboard, and the instrument acquired a fifth course. By the 16th century the classic form of the lute was established, with its six courses of strings (the top course a single string) tuned to G–c–f–a–d´–g´, beginning with the second G below middle C. Playing technique was systematized, and the music was written in tablature (a system of notation in which a staff of horizontal lines represented the courses of the lute), and letters or figures placed on the lines denoted the fret to be stopped and the strings to be plucked by the right hand.

By 1600 the great Bolognese and Venetian schools of lute makers had arisen, including Laux and Sigismond Maler, Hans Frei, Nikolaus Schonfeld, and the Tieffenbruckers. By the fine workmanship and tonal proportions of their instruments, they contributed much to the popularity of the lute and paved the way for its extensive and noble literature of solo music (fantasias, dance movements, song arrangements), song accompaniments, and ensemble music by such composers as Luis Milán and John Dowland.

OTHER STRINGED INSTRUMENTS

After about 1600, French lutenists began to introduce modified tunings. At the same time, the lute itself was altered by the addition of bass strings, or diapasons, which required the enlargement of the neck and head of the instrument. These modified instruments were known as archlutes and included the chitarrone and the theorbo.

THEORBO

The theorbo, a large bass lute (or archlute), was used from the 16th to the 18th century for song accompaniments and for basso continuo parts (an improvised accompaniment on a bass line). It had six to eight single strings running along the fingerboard and, alongside them, eight off-the-fingerboard bass strings (diapasons). Both sets of strings had separate pegboxes connected by an S curve in the instrument's neck. On 18th-century theorbos all but the two top courses of strings were double.

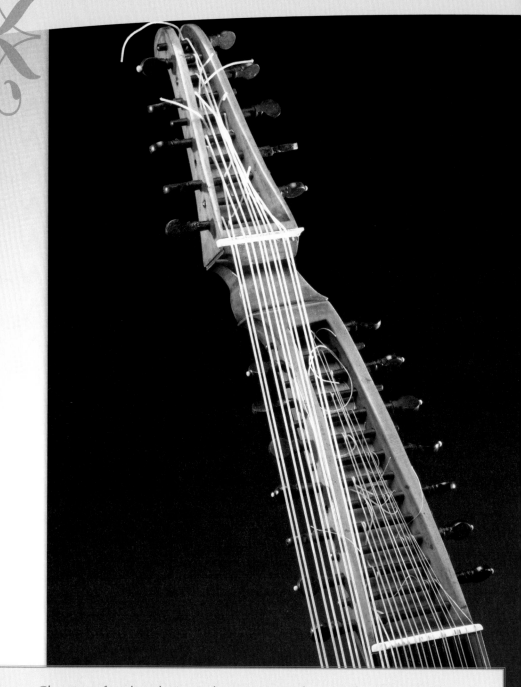

Closeup of a theorbo's neck, strings, pegbox, and tuning pegs. Two sets of six to eight strings were the norm for this instrument, which was essentially a bass lute. Science & Society Picture Library/Getty Images

A similar, smaller instrument, the theorbo-lute, or French lute, was a modification of the regular double-strung lute, to which were added one to three off-the-fingerboard courses of bass strings. There were two pegboxes, one angled backward. Smaller and more agile than the theorbo, the theorbo-lute was the favourite of the 17th-century school of French lutenists; through them, it influenced the style of French harpsichord music.

REBEC

The rebec was a bowed, stringed musical instrument of European medieval and early Renaissance music. It was originally called a *rubebe*, developed about the 11th century from the similar Arab *rabāb*, and was carried to Spain with Muslim culture. Like the *rabāb*, the rebec had a shallow, pear-shaped body, but on the rebec the *rabāb*'s skin belly was replaced by wood and a fingerboard was added. The rebec was held against the chest or chin or, occasionally, with the bottom of the instrument resting on the seated player's left thigh. The three strings were tuned in fifths (e.g., g–d´–a´).

The medieval rebec was apparently a treble instrument, but by the late 15th century rebecs were made in sizes from treble to bass. The family of rebecs was superseded by the viols during the 16th century. The treble rebec survived into the 18th century as the kit, the dancing master's fiddle. The lira and its Balkan folk variants, the *gusla* and *gadulka*, are closely related to the rebec.

VIOL

Also called the viola da gamba, the viol is a bowed, stringed musical instrument used principally in chamber music of the 16th to the 18th century. The viol shares with the

Renaissance lute the tuning of its six strings (two fourths, a major third, two fourths) and the gut frets on its neck. It was made in three sizes: treble, tenor, and bass, with the bottom string tuned, respectively, to d, G (or A), and D. To these sizes was later added the violone, a double bass viol often tuned an octave below the bass.

Viols are characterized by sloping shoulders; deep ribs; thin, flat backs; and, above all, a vertical playing position, with the bottom of the instrument resting on the knee or held between the legs—hence *viola da gamba* (Italian: "leg viol"). The breadth of the bridge, which was arched to give the bow separate access to each string, made forceful playing impossible, and the supine position of the bow hand, palm uppermost, encouraged a smooth playing style. The frets gave to each note the clarity of an open string—a clear, ringing, penetrating tone that was much prized.

By the second half of the 16th century the viol acquired a significant repertory of music for ensemble, for solo bass, and for the lyra viol, a small bass viol (also called *viola bastarda*). But as the style of instrumental composition changed during the 17th century, an expressive, vocal sound in the soprano register was emphasized, and the tenor and treble viols declined in favour of the violin, with which they were unable to compete because their deep bodies created a hollow, nasal timbre.

The bass viol, however, had by the mid-16th century developed a repertory of complex solo divisions, or ornate variations on a melody, often played on a small bass called a division viol. When that fashion died out in the late 1600s, the normal-sized solo bass viol, or viola da gamba (the name became synonymous with the bass viol as the other viols fell into disuse), was used in the instrumental forms of the Baroque period. Solo bass-viol playing continued in Germany and France into the 18th century.

PERCUSSION INSTRUMENTS

In general, percussion instruments belong to either of two groups, idiophones or membranophones. Idiophones are instruments whose own substance vibrates to produce sound (as opposed to the strings of a guitar or the air column of a flute); examples include bells, clappers, and rattles. Membranophones emit sound by the vibration of a stretched membrane. Prime examples of membranophones are drums. The term *percussion instrument* refers to the fact that most idiophones and membranophones are sounded by being struck, although other playing methods include rubbing, shaking, plucking, and scraping.

Although many idiophones and some membranophones are tunable and hence may be melody instruments, both groups serve typically to delineate or emphasize rhythm. The term *percussion instrument* dates to 1619, when the German

Some of the percussion instruments of the modern Western orchestra (clockwise, from top): *xylophone, gong, bass drum, snare drum, and timpani.* Encyclopædia Britannica, Inc.

music theorist and composer Michael Praetorius wrote of *percussa, klopfende Instrument* (German *klopfen,* "to beat"), as any struck instrument, including struck chordophones (stringed instruments). The same combination, including prebow chordophones, constituted the *divisio rhythmica* in the 7th-century *Etymologiae* of Isidore, archbishop of Sevilla (Seville).

Before the Renaissance such instruments as clappers (flat pieces of bone or wood clapped together) were used to keep the rhythm of a dance. Castanets were played in Spain, and cymbals were used in the celebration of many festivities. Bells, too, were a part of daily life and were thought to possess the power to avert evil, thus the practice of attaching bells to clothing and jewelry.

The Renaissance saw the introduction of a number of idiophones, including the xylophone and tuned musical glasses, from the latter of which American statesman Benjamin Franklin would later produce the glass harmonica. By the Renaissance, Europe had a variety of drums performing specialized functions: frame drums and small tabors accompanied dance and song; larger tabors served as time beaters in small mixed ensembles; great cylinder drums with fifes were placed at the disposal of foot troops; large kettledrums and trumpets were restricted to cavalry and ceremonial music of the aristocracy.

Elsewhere the bass viol survived chiefly because its sustained tone lent a pleasing support to the harpsichord. This combination, using the basso continuo, or thorough bass, technique, provided harmonic support for the Baroque instrumental ensemble. When composers in the newer Classical style began to write complete harmonies in the upper instrumental parts, the viol, deprived of its last useful function, dropped out of use altogether. In the

20th century viols were successfully revived for the performance of Renaissance and Baroque music.

ORGAN

Another of the main instruments of the Renaissance was the organ, a keyboard instrument operated by the player's hands and feet in which pressurized air produces notes through a series of pipes organized in scalelike rows. The term *organ* is usually understood to refer to pipe organs. Although it is one of the most complex of all musical instruments, the organ has the longest and most involved history and the largest and oldest extant repertoire of any instrument in Western music.

The earliest history of the organ is so buried in antiquity as to be mere speculation. The earliest surviving record is of the Greek engineer Ctesibius, who lived in Alexandria in the 3rd century BCE. He is credited with the invention of an organ that made use of an ingenious principle, though it was applicable only to a very small instrument. A piston pump operated by a lever supplied air to a reservoir. At its upper end, this reservoir communicated directly with the windchest. The reservoir, cylindrical in shape and with no bottom, was placed in a large drum-shaped container that was partly filled with water. As the reservoir became filled with air, the air would escape around its lower edge. In this way a more or less equal pressure of air was maintained inside the reservoir. This type of organ, with the wind regulated by water pressure, is called a hydraulus. It may have served chiefly as a noisemaker or an engineering marvel. Little is known of any music that might have been played on it. A clay model of a hydraulus was discovered in 1885 in the ruins of Carthage (near modern Tunis, Tunisia), and the remains of an actual instrument were found in 1931 at Aquincum, near Budapest.

The first recorded appearance of an exclusively bellow-fed organ, however, was not until almost 400 years later. By the 8th century organs were being built in Europe, and from the 10th century their association with the church had been established. The 15th and 16th centuries witnessed significant tonal and mechanical advances and the emergence of national schools of organ building. By the early 17th century all the essential elements of the instrument had been developed, and subsequent developments involved either tonal changes or technological refinements.

During the Middle Ages and the Renaissance, three diminutive forms of the organ were widely used. These were, first, the positive (in which category are included most chamber organs of the period), a small organ capable of being moved, usually by two men, either on carrying poles or on a cart. The second type, the portative, was smaller still, with only one set of pipes and a manual of very short compass. It was carried by the player, who worked the bellows with one hand and played the keys with the other. Such instruments were used in processions and possibly in concerted instrumental ensembles. Between the last two in size was the third type, the regal, or reed organ, a small, easily portable pipe organ usually having only a single set, or rank, of reed pipes. The beating reeds are surmounted by small resonators, producing a nasal, buzzing tone. Wind under pressure to sound the pipes is supplied by one or two bellows attached to the instrument and operated by the player or an assistant.

STRINGED KEYBOARD INSTRUMENTS

Though they share one feature—a keyboard—with the organ, stringed keyboard instruments were not themselves developed until the 14th century. Among the many varieties of this type of instrument, the clavichord, harpsichord, spinet, and virginal were most characteristic of the Renaissance.

The earliest known reference to a stringed keyboard instrument dates from 1360, when an instrument called the *eschiquier* was mentioned in account books of John II the Good, king of France. The *eschiquier* was described in 1388 as "resembling an organ that sounds by means of strings." There exists no more complete description of the *eschiquier*, however, and it is not known whether the instrument was a variety of clavichord, in which the strings are struck by blades of metal that must remain in contact with them as long as they are to sound; a harpsichord, in which the strings are plucked; or a type of keyboard-equipped dulcimer, in which—as in the piano—the strings are struck by small hammers that immediately rebound from them. All three types of instruments were described and illustrated about 1440 by Henri Arnaut of Zwolle, personal physician of Philip the Good, duke of Burgundy.

Despite the uncertainty regarding the *eschiquier*, it seems probable that the clavichord was the earliest stringed instrument having keys that could be pushed down by the fingers. The term *clavichord* first appears in a German document from 1404, and the instrument is recognizable in a German altar carving from 1425. Its principle of operation resembles that of the medieval organistrum, and it is apparently closely related to the monochord, an instrument consisting of a shallow closed box over which one or two strings were stretched and supported by movable bridges. The monochord was in continuous use by theorists from ancient Greece onward as a device for explaining and measuring musical intervals. The kinship of the clavichord to the monochord was so close that,

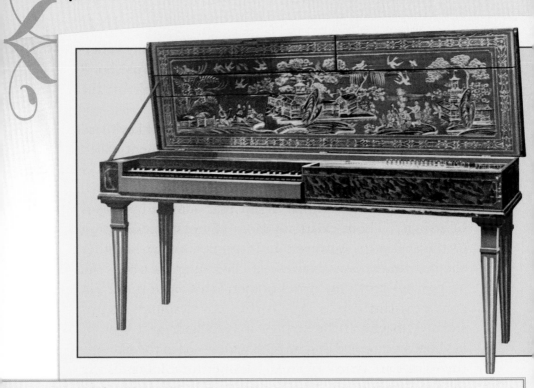

Artist's rendering of a clavichord, a forerunner of the modern piano. Clavichords typically sported lavish painted and/or inlaid artwork on their lids and cases. Buyenlarge/Archive Photos/Getty Images

as late as the 16th century, clavichords were often called *monocordia*.

CLAVICHORD

The clavichord is usually rectangular in shape, and its case and lid were usually highly decorated, painted, and inlaid. The right, or treble, end contains the soundboard, the bridge, and the wrest, or tuning, pins. The strings run horizontally from the tuning pins over the bridge to the hitch pins in the left, or bass, end, where felt strips woven through the strings act as dampers. A small brass blade, the tangent, stands on each key just below its string. When the key is depressed, the tangent strikes the string, dividing it into two parts. It thus both determines the vibrating length of the string and causes it to sound. The string segment between the tangent and bridge vibrates, producing a note; the left part is damped by the felt. When the key is released, the tangent falls away from the string, which is then silenced by the felt.

Alone among the forerunners of the piano, the clavichord can achieve dynamic variation—piano, forte, crescendo, diminuendo—by the player's touch alone. It can produce vibrato, or *Bebung*, if finger pressure on the key is varied. Its tone is silvery and soft, and it proved to be best suited for intimate music such as Carl Philipp Emanuel Bach's keyboard sonatas and fantasias.

Because it arises directly from the way in which the sound of the instrument is produced, the softness of the instrument cannot readily be overcome. It is impossible to impart very much energy to a string by striking it at one end (it is for this reason that a guitarist makes less sound when he strikes the strings against the fingerboard with his left hand than when he plucks them with his right, even though the pitches produced are the same). In compensation, the clavichordist alone of all keyboard-instrument players has control over a note once it has been struck. As long as a note is sounding, the player has contact with the string through the tangent and key, and by changing pressure on the key one can vary the pitch of the note, produce a controlled vibrato, or even create the illusion of prolonging or swelling the tone. Although the maximum loudness of which a clavichord is capable is not great, its softest pianissimo is very soft indeed, and the clavichordist controls an infinite number of gradations in loudness between these two extremes.

The quiet tone of the clavichord made it impractical to use the instrument in ensemble music, except for providing a discreet accompaniment for a flutist or a singer. Although much of the solo keyboard music of the 16th–18th centuries can be played on the clavichord, it cannot be stated that much of it before the latter part of the 18th century was especially composed with the clavichord in mind.

HARPSICHORD

The strings of the harpsichord are set in vibration by plucking. It was one of the most important keyboard instruments in European music from the 16th through the first half of the 18th century.

Generally, the harpsichord has two or more sets of strings, each of which produces different tone qualities. One set may sound an octave higher than the others and is called a 4-foot register, whereas a set of strings at normal pitch is called an 8-foot register. In some 20th-century harpsichords, a 16-foot register, sounding an octave lower, is added, but this addition was extremely rare in old harpsichords. Two sets of 8-foot strings may produce distinct tone quality because they are plucked at different points or with plectra (picks) made of different material.

The earliest surviving harpsichords were built in Italy in the early 16th century. Little is known of the early history of the harpsichord, but, during the 16th–18th century, it underwent considerable evolution and became one of the most important European instruments. Most of the great Baroque composers played or wrote for the harpsichord.

SPINET

A small form of the harpsichord, the spinet is generally wing-shaped, with a single set of strings placed at an

PSALTERY

A precursor of the harpsichord, the psaltery has plucked strings of gut, horsehair, or metal stretched across a flat soundboard, often trapezoidal but also rectangular, triangular, or wing-shaped. The strings are open, none being stopped to produce different notes. The instrument, probably of Middle Eastern origin in late Classical times, reached Europe in the 12th century as a variety of the trapezoidal Arabic psaltery, or *qānūn*. It was popular in Europe until about the 15th century and developed there into several shapes, including the characteristic "boar's head"—i.e., with two incurving sides. It was plucked with the fingers or quill plectra. Even after its decline, it continued to be played on occasion in fashionable society. It also gave rise to the harpsichord, which is a large psaltery with a keyboard mechanism for plucking the strings.

Angel playing a psaltery, detail from Angel Musicians, *panel by Hans Memling; in the Koninklijk Museum voor Schone Kunsten, Antwerp, Belgium.* Courtesy of the Koninklijk Museum voor Schone Kunsten, Antwerp

The medieval *qānūn* also diffused eastward across India to Indonesia and China. Still prominent in the music of Arabic-speaking countries, it is played with finger plectra and is normally triple strung.

oblique angle to the keyboard. The wing-shaped spinet may have originated in Italy during the 16th century. It later became known in France and England.

Spinets were popular substitutes for the larger, more expensive harpsichords and were made in large numbers during the late 17th and 18th centuries, especially in England. Their cases were often highly ornamented and decorated. The name *spinet* may derive from the Latin *spinae* ("thorns"), perhaps reflecting the shape of the tiny quills or leather wedges that pluck the strings. In modern usage, *spinet* commonly refers to a short form of upright piano.

VIRGINAL

Another musical instrument of the harpsichord family, the virginal (also called virginals) may be the oldest member. It may take its name from Latin *virga* ("rod"), referring to the jacks, or wooden shafts that rest on the ends of the keys and hold the plucking mechanism.  Unlike the harpsichord and spinet, the virginal's single set of strings runs nearly parallel to the keyboard. By building the instrument with its keyboard at one side or the other of the front of the rectangular case, different tone colours can be obtained because of the change in plucking point of the string.

English virginal (with jack rail removed) made by Robert Hatley, London, 1664. The Benton-Fletcher Collection at the National Trust Property, Fenton House, Hampstead, London

Italian virginals, often polygonal in shape, differed from the rectangular Flemish and English virginals in having the keyboard centrally placed, thus producing a characteristic mellow tone. Sometimes two virginals were built together, a small one fitting like a drawer into the case of the larger. The smaller played at a higher pitch and could sometimes be mounted over the keys of the larger virginal so that one player could control both. Virginals were particularly popular in 16th- and 17th-century England, where the name was also used generically to mean any harpsichord.

ASSORTED WIND INSTRUMENTS

The growing separation of instrumental from vocal music and the development of polyphony in the Renaissance demanded the building of instruments in different sizes for the various parts in order to secure a smooth blend throughout the texture. The ensembles using such a blend of instruments were called consorts. Wind instruments flourished. At no time in the history of music was the choice of available timbres greater, and within the 16th century as many instruments as possible were built in families. The common sizes, built a fifth apart, were called the treble, tenor, and bass, usually with corresponding pitches in winds of A, D, and G. Flutes and recorders were an octave higher. A descant and a great bass were introduced for music that exceeded the combined range of the standard instruments. Woodwinds, in general, were made in one piece in a plain design, and Venice appears to have been an early centre of wind-instrument manufacture.

The new concept of blending tone quality was applied to the flutes and recorders. Both were made with a relatively large cylindrical bore. As a result, the upper range was limited, but the effective octave and a half that remained was sufficient for Renaissance music. Since the transverse

SERPENT

The serpent is a bass wind instrument sounded by the vibration of the lips against a cup mouthpiece. It was probably invented in 1590 by Edme Guillaume, a French canon of Auxerre, as an improvement on bass versions of the closely related cornett. It is made of wood in a serpentine curve 7 to 8 feet (2 to 2.5 metres) long, and it has a conical bore and six finger holes. Originally it accompanied plainchant (Gregorian chant) in churches. The serpent possessed a rich tone and wide dynamic range. It was the instrument of several early 19th-century virtuosos and was sometimes used in orchestras. In about 1800, keys were added, extending the player's reach and allowing higher notes to be produced. Metal serpents also appeared, as did bassoon-shaped versions. Serpents were played in some Spanish bands as late as 1884 and in a few rural French churches on into the early 20th century.

flute (held sideways and to the right of the player) adapted less well to various sizes, it was more often used with other instruments.

Double reeds were particularly numerous during the Renaissance, and in many species the reeds were capped. The best known of these was the crumhorn, an instrument of narrow cylindrical bore whose unusual J shape complemented its pungent, buzzy tone. The cap made it impossible for a player to exert lip pressure on the large reed within, so the instrument could not be overblown. Its seven finger holes, one thumbhole, and one upper key gave a range of only nine notes. Nevertheless, the crumhorn consort made an excellent ensemble, and some fine early sets of instruments still survive as testimony.

Shawms were a particularly important family of loud double reeds, with related instruments spread across all Asia. Their wide conical bore, large double reed, and seven front finger holes provided them with a loud, reedy tone. The player could rest his lips on a wooden pirouette into which the reed was inserted and activate the reed without contact in the wind chamber formed in his mouth. Nevertheless, the reed could be controlled if desired, and the instrument was overblown partly through the second octave. Shawms were made in progressive sizes, the bass attaining a length of about 2.5 metres (8 to 9 feet). The power of the shawms enabled them to consort with trombones and to carry well in the outdoor tower music of central European cities.

The more gentle curtal was a noncapped double reed with its conical bore doubled back within the same block and ending in a small bell. It was activated by a long, carefully trimmed double reed connected with the instrument proper by a short tube called the *bocal*. Six front finger holes, two thumbholes, and two keys gave it a range of two octaves and a second. It was first mentioned in 1540, and its bass (sometimes called the double curtal) soon became the most important size. The double reeds with doubled back cylindrical bores were an interesting development. The *sordone* (French *courtaut*) was such an instrument, its narrow bore terminating in a side vent near the *bocal*. Most extraordinary was the rackett, whose narrow bore went through a cylinder of ivory or wood as many as nine times to make a double-bass instrument from a cylinder length of a few inches. The instrument plays an octave below notation and forms the lowest of the Renaissance winds. The Renaissance reeds that were not adaptable to outdoor music vanished early in the 17th century, except for the curtal. The shawm survived somewhat longer in the West and remained important in the East.

Another important woodwind was the *cornetto* (an Italian name Anglicized as cornett; also known under its German name, *Zink*), the descendant of the medieval cow's horn with finger holes. The treble cornett in g was made from two pieces of wood, hollowed out and glued together to create a mildly conical tube, usually octagonal and most often curved in the shape of its prototype. A covering of leather, protecting the surface and sealing any leaks, was frequently decorated at the upper end. The cornett was made in larger sizes, but they were not widely used.

The sackbut (from Old French *saqueboute*, meaning "pull-push") was an early form of trombone invented in the 15th century, probably in Burgundy. It has thicker walls than the modern trombone, imparting a softer tone, and its bell is narrower. It was found to blend nicely in consort with cornetts as the treble instrument or in the loud consort in the company of shawms.

The sackbut answered the need for a lower-pitched trumpet that composers of the time sought. Its telescoping slide mechanism is retained in the modern trombone.

CHAPTER 3

EARLY RENAISSANCE COMPOSERS

Among the late medieval and early Renaissance composers can be counted a number of innovators who provided the foundations for the whole of Renaissance music. Whatever their particular origins, they were usually associated with a court—often more than one over the course of a lifetime—having as options for their support only the church or noble patrons.

JOHN DUNSTABLE

(b. c. 1385, Eng.—d. Dec. 24, 1453, London)

English composer John Dunstable had a notable influence on the transition between late medieval and early Renaissance music. The influence of his sweet, sonorous music was recognized by his contemporaries on the Continent, including Martin le Franc, who wrote in his *Champion des dames* (c. 1440) that the leading composers of the day, Guillaume Dufay and Binchois, owed their superiority to what they learned from Dunstable's "English manner."

Information about Dunstable's life is scanty. He was in the service of the duke of Bedford, who was regent of France from 1422 to 1435 and military opponent of Joan of Arc. Dunstable probably accompanied his patron to

France. His music was well known on the Continent. His epitaph referred to him as skilled in mathematics and astronomy as well as in music.

Dunstable's influence on European music is seen in his flowing, gently asymmetrical rhythms and, above all, in his harmonies. He represents a culmination of the English tradition of full, sonorous harmonies based on the third and sixth that persisted through the 14th century alongside the starker, more dissonant style of Continental music.

Dunstable left about 60 works, including mass sections, motets, and secular songs; they are largely written for three parts. In the cantus firmus tenors of some of his mass sections he frequently used the Continental device of isorhythm (rhythmic patterns overlapped with melodic patterns of different length). In many of his works the treble line (the highest voice part), rather than the tenor line, dominates. It may be freely composed, or it may carry an ornamented version of the cantus firmus, an English innovation. Some of Dunstable's motets show double structure: building the polyphonic composition on two melodies, a plainchant cantus firmus in the tenor and a melody in the treble that appears with variations. This structure, which may have been invented by Dunstable, became popular with later composers.

GUILLAUME DUFAY

(b. c. 1400 – d. Nov. 27, 1474, Cambrai, Bishopric of Cambrai [France])

French composer Guillaume Dufay (or Du Fay) was chorister at the Cambrai Cathedral (1409), entered the service of Carlo Malatesta of Rimini c. 1420, and in 1428 joined the papal singers. In 1426 he became a canon of Cambrai. After seven years in the service of the duke of Savoy, Dufay lived at Cambrai from about 1440 and

CHANSON

The French art song of the Middle Ages and the Renaissance is called the chanson. Those that were written before 1500 are preserved mostly in large manuscript collections called chansonniers.

Dating back to the 12th century, the monophonic chanson reached its greatest popularity with the trouvères of the 13th century, and can still be found in the mid-14th-century lais (a verse-song form) of the composer and poet Guillaume de Machaut. These monophonic chansons show the development of intricate musico-poetic forms deriving from the songs of the slightly earlier counterparts of the trouvères, the troubadours. These forms were eventually simplified to become the *formes fixes* ("fixed forms") of the accompanied chanson.

The accompanied chanson—for a solo voice with written parts for one or more accompanying instruments—dominated French song until the end of the 15th century. Almost all accompanied chansons adhere to one of the three *formes fixes*: ballade, rondeau, or *virelai*. The style is sophisticated, and the songs are evidently written for a court audience with high artistic aspirations and a cultivated taste. The general subject matter was courtly love, which entailed a highly conventionalized code of behaviours.

The chanson for vocal ensemble had several antecedents. A chanson designed for two or three had appeared; about 1460 the polytextual chanson was in evidence, with two or more singers singing different texts simultaneously. By the end of the 15th century composers were beginning to look to a new kind of chanson texture. The work of the Flemish composer Josquin des Prez shows the gradual change to a style of chanson with four voices singing the same text, sometimes in melodic imitation but also in a homophonic (chordal) style.

In the next century the four-voice style gave way to five and six. The later years of the 16th century saw the perfection of the polyphonic (multipart, usually with interwoven melodic lines) chanson in the work of Orlando di Lasso. After 1600 the chanson yielded to a new kind of song: the *air de cour* for solo voice with lute accompaniment.

supervised the music of the cathedral. He took a degree in canon law about 1445 and in 1446 became a canon of Mons. Dufay's surviving works include 87 motets, 59 French chansons, seven Italian chansons, seven complete masses, and 35 mass sections. He often used, and may have originated, the technique of *fauxbourdon*, a musical texture produced by three voices proceeding primarily in parallel motion in intervals corresponding to the first inversion of the triad. The result was a particularly "sweet" sound in contrast to the mixture of passing dissonants and open sonorities favoured in earlier music.

During his Italian period Dufay composed a number of ceremonial motets for public celebrations, among them the election of Pope Eugenius IV (1431), the Treaty of Viterbo (1433), and the dedication of Italian architect Filippo Brunelleschi's dome for Sta. Maria del Fiore, Florence (1436). For the brilliant Feast of the Pheasant held in 1454 by Philip the Good of Burgundy and intended to initiate a crusade to recapture Jerusalem, Dufay composed a lamentation for the Church in Constantinople.

Dufay's chansons, usually written for three voices, deal with subjects such as springtime, love, and melancholy. Most use the poetic-musical forms of the ballade, rondeau, and *virelai*. A few are written in freer form.

Guillame Dufay (left), pictured with fellow composer Gilles Binochois, in an illustration from French writer Martin le Franc's Le Champion des Dames, 1440. Bibliotheque Nationale de Paris/Giraudon/The Bridgeman Art Library

Dufay's masses laid the foundation for the rapid musical development of the mass in the second half of the 15th century. His complete mass settings are in four voices and use a cantus firmus placed in the tenor line. His canti firmi include secular songs such as *L'homme armé* (used by many composers up to Palestrina) and his own ballade *Se la face ay pale*, and sacred melodies such as *Ave Regina coelorum*.

In these and other works of his Cambrai period Dufay perfected a graceful and expressive style that incorporated into Continental music the sweet harmonies of the *contenance angloise* or "English manner" that Martin le Franc's *Le Champion des Dames* attributed to John Dunstable. Dufay's music created the characteristic style of the Burgundian composers that links late medieval music with the style of later Franco-Flemish composers of the Renaissance.

BINCHOIS

(b. c. 1400, Mons, Hainaut [now in Belgium]—d. Sept. 20, 1460, Soignies, near Mons)

The Flemish composer Gilles de Binche (de Bins) was known as Binchois (Binchoys). He wrote both church music and secular chansons that were among the finest of their genre, being notable for their elegance of line and grave sweetness of expression. The upper voice in Binchois's mostly three-part songs is considered to be particularly lyrical.

Gilles's father, Jean de Binche, was connected to the court of Hainaut. Binchois was in Paris in 1424 serving William de la Pole, earl (later duke) of Suffolk, and returned with him to Hainaut in 1425. In 1430 Binchois joined the chapel of Philip III (the Good) of Burgundy, where he remained until his death, eventually becoming second chaplain and cantor. The Burgundian court was in most ways the predominant court of the region, and it was equated by those who enjoyed the duke's patronage with the court of Alexander the Great. Binchois was joined there by the likes of fellow composer Guillaume Dufay and Flemish painter Jan van Eyck, who is believed to have painted a portrait of Binchois. By 1437 Binchois had become canon at Mons, Soignies, and Cassel.

In both his sacred and secular music, Binchois cultivated the gently subtle rhythm, the suavely graceful melody, and the smooth treatment of dissonance of his English contemporaries. The lyrics to many of his songs were poems by many of the best-known poets of the day, including Charles, duc d'Orléans, and Christine de Pisan. His music, especially that of his chansons, was widely known and has been shown to be the basis of works by other composers. A landmark 1957 edition of Binchois's secular music (since amended) was edited by Wolfgang Rehm, and *The Sacred Music of Gilles Binchois*, edited by Philip Kaye, was published in 1992.

JEAN DE OCKEGHEM

(b. c. 1410 — d. Feb. 6, 1497, Tours, France[?])

Jean de Ockeghem (d'Okeghem) is considered to be one of the great masters of the Franco-Flemish style that dominated European Renaissance music. Ockeghem's earliest recorded appointment was as a singer at Antwerp Cathedral (1443–44). He served similarly in the chapel of Charles, duke de Bourbon (1446–48), and later in the royal chapel. He was chaplain and composer to three successive French kings, Charles VII, Louis XI, and Charles VIII. As treasurer of the wealthy Abbey of Saint-Martin at Tours, he received a handsome salary. Like many of his Flemish contemporaries he traveled widely and used his visits to distant cities to extend his musical knowledge. As a teacher he had great influence on the following generation of composers. His death was mourned in writing by Dutch humanist and scholar Desiderius Erasmus, whose text was set to music by Johannes Lupi. *A Déploration* by French poet and chronicler Jean Molinet was set to music by the great Franco-Flemish composer Josquin des Prez.

Illustration depicting a choir singing the Gloria, conducted by Jean de Ockeghem (front left). DEA Picture Library/De Agostini/Getty Images

Ockeghem's surviving works include 14 masses, 10 motets, and 20 chansons. His work sounds richer than that of his predecessors Guillaume Dufay and John Dunstable. During Ockeghem's era the instrumentally supported vocal lines of earlier music were gradually modified to make way for sonorous choral harmony. The bass range in Ockeghem's compositions extends lower than in his predecessors' music, and the tenor and countertenor voices cross in and out of each other, creating a heavier texture. The long melodic lines of the different voices cadence in different places so that a continuous flow of music results. Melodic imitation occurs here and there but is not prominent. His *Missa prolationum* and *Missa cuiusvis toni* are examples of his highly developed contrapuntal and canonic technique, but the strict device of canon, of which he was a master, is subtly used and is rarely apparent to the listener. He frequently used preexistent material as a device for musical unity.

Ockeghem's 10 motets include Marian texts, such as *Ave Maria*, *Salve regina*, and *Alma redemptoris mater*, and a complete setting of the responsory *Gaude Maria*. Unlike other composers of the early 15th century, he wrote his masses in a style more solemn than that of his secular music.

JAKOB OBRECHT

(b. Nov. 22, 1452, Bergen-op-Zoom, Brabant [now in the Netherlands]—d. 1505, Ferrara [Italy])

Jakob Obrecht (Hobrecht) was one of the leading composers in the preeminently vocal and contrapuntal Franco-Flemish style. He was the son of Willem Obrecht, a trumpeter. His first known appointment was in 1484 as instructor of choirboys at Cambrai Cathedral, where he was criticized for negligence in caring for the boys. In

1485 he became assistant choirmaster of the cathedral at Brugge. According to Swiss humanist and music theorist Henricus Glareanus, Desiderius Erasmus was among the choirboys at one of Obrecht's positions. In 1487 Obrecht visited Italy, where he met Ercole I, duke of Ferrara, an admirer of his music. The duke installed Obrecht in Ferrara and sought a papal appointment for him there. The appointment was not forthcoming, and Obrecht returned to Bergen-op-Zoom in 1488. In 1504 he again traveled to Ferrara, where he died of plague.

Obrecht's compositional style is notable for its warm, graceful melodies and its clear harmonies that approach a modern feeling for tonality. His surviving works include 27 masses, 19 motets, and 31 secular pieces.

His masses are largely for four voices. Most employ a cantus firmus taken from plainchant or from a secular song. His use of the cantus firmus varies from the customary statement of it in the tenor to fragments of it in each movement and in voices other than the tenor. Some of his late masses employ what is called parody technique — using all voices of a preexistent chanson or motet, rather than a single borrowed melody, as a unifying device.

His motets are largely to texts in honour of the Virgin Mary (e.g., *Salve Regina*; *Alma Redemptoris Mater*). They characteristically have the cantus firmus melody placed in the tenor in long notes. Some of his motets are polytextual — that is, different parts sang different texts — a rather outdated practice. More progressive is his use of melodic imitation and his frequent consecutive tenths.

JOSQUIN DES PREZ

(b. c. 1450, Condé-sur-l'Escaut?, Burgundian Hainaut [France] — d. Aug. 27, 1521, Condé-sur-l'Escaut)

Josquin des Prez, drawing by Joris van der Straeten, 16th century. The Bettmann Archive

Josquin des Prez (Desprez, des Prés, Després) is commonly considered one of the greatest, if not the greatest, of the Renaissance composers. His early life has been the subject of much scholarly debate, and the first solid evidence of his work comes from a roll of musicians associated with the cathedral in Cambrai in the early 1470s. During the late 1470s and early '80s, he sang for the courts of René I of Anjou and Duke Galeazzo Maria Sforza of Milan, and from 1486 to about 1494 he performed for the papal chapel. Sometime between then and 1499, when he became choirmaster to Duke Ercole I of Ferrara, he apparently had connections with the Chapel Royal of Louis XII of France and with the cathedral of Cambrai. In Ferrara he wrote, in honour of his employer, the mass *Hercules Dux Ferrariae*, and his motet *Miserere* was composed at the duke's request. He seems to have left Ferrara on the death of the duke in 1505 and later became provost of the collegiate church of Notre Dame in Condé.

Josquin's compositions fall into the three principal categories of motets, masses, and chansons. Of the 20 masses that survive complete, 17 were printed in his lifetime in three sets (1502, 1505, 1514) by Italian music printer Ottaviano dei Petrucci. His motets and chansons were included in other Petrucci publications, from the *Odhecaton* (an anthology of popular chansons) of 1501 onward, and in collections of other printers. Musical laments on his death by Nicolas Gombert and other contemporary composers are extant. The German religious leader Martin Luther expressed great admiration for Josquin's music, calling him "master of the notes, which must do as he wishes; other composers must do as the notes wish." In his musical techniques Josquin stands at the summit of the Renaissance, blending traditional forms with innovations that later became standard practices. The expressiveness of his music marks a break with the medieval tradition of more abstract music.

In his motets, particularly, Josquin gave free reign to his talent, expressing sorrow in poignant harmonies, employing suspension for emphasis, and taking the voices gradually into their lowest registers when the text speaks of death. Josquin used the old cantus firmus style, but he also developed the motet style that characterized the 16th century after him. His motets, as do his masses, show an approach to the modern sense of tonality.

In his chansons Josquin was the principal exponent of a style new in the mid-15th century, in which the learned

COUNTERPOINT IN THE RENAISSANCE

The Renaissance composer was concerned primarily with melodic relationships between the voice parts. The predominant technique used was that of imitation; i.e., the successive statement of the same or similar melody in each of the voice parts so that one voice imitates another.

Imitation had appeared earlier in the Italian *caccia* and French *chace*, roundlike vocal forms of the 14th century, and in England in the 13th-century round, *Sumer is icumen in*. These compositions anticipate the Renaissance and also emphasize the rhythmic relationships typical of medieval counterpoint.

During the Renaissance the technique of imitation contributed to a new unity between the voices. Renaissance composers strove also for clear melodic relationships between voices. Consequently imitations usually began on the same beat of a measure and were separated in pitch by simple intervals such as the fifth (as, C–G) or octave (as, C–C). The Renaissance theorists, among them Johannes Tinctoris and Gioseffo Zarlino, categorized dissonances according to type and governed each type by definite rhythmic and melodic restrictions.

What is often proclaimed as the "golden age" of counterpoint—meaning melodic counterpoint—stretches from the late 15th to the late 16th century, from the Flemish master Jean de Ockeghem to the Spanish Tomás Luis de Victoria and the Elizabethan William Byrd. Its leading masters were Josquin des Prez, Giovanni Pierluigi da Palestrina, and Orlando di Lasso. The northern composers in particular showed a penchant for complex melodic relationships. Ockeghem's *Missa prolationum* (*Prolation Mass*), for example, involves simultaneous canons in two pairs of voices. (In a canon, one melody is derived from another. It may be identical, as in a round, or it may be given various alterations, as of speed, or metre or omission of certain notes.) The most versatile craftsman of the Renaissance was Josquin, whose music displays a continual variety of contrapuntal ingenuities, including melodic imitation. His use of successive imitation in several voices is coupled with melodic smoothness and rhythmic vitality.

The imitative style came to its fullest flowering in the late 16th century not only in the masses and motets of di Lasso and Palestrina but also in secular songs such as the French chanson and Italian madrigal. It also flourished in instrumental music in such contrapuntal forms as fantasias, canzonas, and ricercari.

techniques of canon and counterpoint were applied to secular song. He abandoned the fixed forms of the rondeau and the ballade, employing freer forms of his own device. Though a few chansons are set chordally rather than polyphonically, a number of others are skilled examples of counterpoint in five or six voices, maintaining sharp rhythms, straightforwardness, and clarity of texture.

HEINRICH ISAAC

(b. c. 1450, Brabant—d. 1517, Florence [Italy])

Heinrich Isaac (Isaak) was one of the leading composers of the Franco-Flemish school in the late 15th century. A pupil of Florentine organist Antonio Squarcialupi, he taught in the household of Lorenzo de' Medici in Florence (c. 1484–92) and set to music some of Lorenzo's own carnival songs. Isaac apparently left Florence during the Medicean exile, entering the service of the emperor Maximilian I about 1494. In 1497 he was appointed court composer. Between 1497 and 1514 he traveled extensively, finally settling in Florence.

Isaac's main publications were a collection of masses (1506) and the posthumous *Choralis Constantinus* (1550–55), one of the few complete polyphonic settings of the Proper of the Mass for all Sundays (and certain other feasts). It also contains five settings of the Ordinary. At least in part the work was commissioned for the diocese of Constance in 1508 and employs plainsongs unique to the Constance liturgy. Isaac left his great monument unfinished; it was completed by his student Ludwig Senfl.

In his sacred music Isaac treats the cantus firmus (fixed melody) resourcefully, placing the chant in any voice or sharing it between two parts, either in long notes or embroidered with shorter notes. He also uses it as a thematic basis for composing contrapuntal imitations, a technique that came to dominate 16th-century music.

He wrote about 40 secular songs. His Italian *frottole* (simply accompanied songs) have charming treble melodies. His polyphonic German lieder normally present the tune in the tenor but, unlike many contemporary lieder, do not cadence into several sections. His famous "Innsbruck, ich muss dich lassen" ("Innsbruck, I must leave you") recalls the style of the simpler *frottola*. This song was later reworked as a chorale, "O Welt ["World"], ich muss dich lassen," familiar through arrangements by Johann Sebastian Bach and by Brahms.

Isaac's *Missa carminum*, motets from *Choralis Constantinus*, music for the court of Lorenzo de' Medici, and secular works *Virgo prudentissima* have been recorded.

LOYSET COMPÈRE

(b. c. 1445, Hainaut? [now in Belgium]—d. Aug. 16, 1518, Saint-Quentin, France)

Loyset Compère was another significant composer of the Franco-Flemish school, best known for his motets and chansons. Little is known of Compère's early life. The French poet and chronicler Jean Molinet, who seems to have known the composer, reported that his family was from Saint-Omer (in France), though it is known that later in life he became a naturalized French citizen. During the mid-1470s Compère was a member of the chapel choir of Galeazzo Maria Sforza, duke of Milan, but, when the duke was murdered in 1477 and the choir was reduced, Compère was among those who were listed to leave the court. By 1486 he was a *chantre ordinaire* in the service of the French king Charles VIII. Compère became a naturalized French citizen in 1494 and probably traveled with Charles during the French invasion of Italy (1494). Compère was subsequently a dean of Saint Géry in Cambrai (1498–1500) and provost at Saint Pierre in Douai (1500–1503/04). An 18th-century history of this period indicates that the composer had earned bachelor's degrees in canon and civil law. He was also canon and chancellor at Saint-Quentin, and his remains are buried in the church there. Throughout his tenure at these churches, he seems to have continued to serve the French court.

Once believed to have learned from Josquin des Prez, Compère is now known to have been older than Josquin by perhaps a decade, and scholars believe that Compère may have pioneered some of the techniques and styles that both composers share. Compère's surviving works include several motets of a variety of types, two *frottole*, more than 50 chansons, two complete masses (*Alles regrets* and *L'Homme armé*), three cycles of *motetti missales* ("substitution masses"), and four complete Magnificats.

PIERRE DE LA RUE

(b. c. 1452, Tournai, Flanders [now in Belgium]—d. Nov. 20, 1518, Courtrai [now Kortrijk, Belgium])

Composer Pierre de La Rue is known by a variety of names. His given name is also spelled Pierchon, Perchon, or Pierson, while his family name is also spelled De La Rue or de la Rue. However one spells his name, he was a dominant composer of religious music in the Flemish, or Netherlandish, style.

Little is known of La Rue's early life. He may have worked first as a part-time singer in Brussels (1469), then perhaps in Ghent (1471–72) and Nieuwpoort (1472–77). From about 1492 he became a member of the chapel of the Habsburg-Burgundian court, in which office he served Maximilian I, Philip the Handsome, and from 1508 Margaret of Austria, regent of the Netherlands. Together with his patrons he visited France and Spain. In 1516 he became canon at Courtrai Cathedral. La Rue left more than 30 masses and about 45 motets, distinguished by their densely compressed style and skillful structure. His 32 surviving secular pieces include vocal part-songs and instrumentally accompanied solos.

JEAN MOUTON

(b. c. 1459, Haut-Wignes, France—d. Oct. 30, 1522, Saint-Quentin)

French composer Jean Mouton made his reputation as a writer of sacred music in the Franco-Flemish style. He was a chorister in Nesle (1477–83) and worked in Amiens and Grenoble from 1500 to 1502 before joining the French royal chapel under Louis XII and Francis I. He apparently studied with Josquin des Prez, and he taught Adriaan Willaert. His music leads away from the older style, which falls into clear sections, and instead emphasizes a continuous flow of vocal lines from beginning to end, with pervasive melodic imitation. He was a master of the canon, a musical form and compositional technique based on the principle of strict imitation, in which an initial melody is imitated at a specified time interval by one or more parts, either at the unison (i.e., the same pitch) or at some other pitch. Mouton produced mainly masses and motets, which were published during his lifetime by printers such as Ottaviano dei Petrucci and Pierre Attaingnant.

CHAPTER 4

LATER RENAISSANCE COMPOSERS ACTIVE IN ITALY

I taly, which was not yet a unified country, was a second centre of musical activity. Not only was it the home of the popes, who had enormous wealth, but it contained the ancient prosperous families of the Este, Borgia, Gonzaga, and Medici.

JACQUES ARCADELT

(b. c. 1504, Liège? [now in Belgium]—d. Oct. 14, 1568, Paris?, France)

Flemish composer Jacques Arcadelt (Jakob Arcadet) was noted for his madrigals. His early style—characterized by sonorous homophony and combined with the texts of such poets as Petrarch, Giovanni Boccaccio, Jacopo Sannazzaro, Pietro Bembo, and Michelangelo—helped establish that musical form as a serious art form. Arcadelt produced several volumes of madrigals, as well as a variety of chansons, masses, motets, and other works.

Arcadelt probably was born in what is now Belgium, though his origins are uncertain. He became a singer as well as a leading composer. During the 1530s he was in Florence and possibly also in Rome. His first known compositions, published in Germany in 1531, were a group of motets in the Florentine style, and he also wrote several

FROTTOLE

The *frottola* (singular) was an Italian secular song popular in the late 15th and early 16th centuries. Usually it was a composition for four voices with the melody in the top line. *Frottole* could be performed by unaccompanied voices or by a solo voice with instrumental accompaniment. The *frottola* had chordal texture and clear-cut rhythm, usually in ¾ or ⁴⁄₄ metre. The voice parts had narrow ranges and frequently repeated voices. Its musical style was simple, in deliberate contrast to the complexity of more sophisticated vocal music of the period. The *frottola*, as it developed by 1530, was the direct antecedent of the 16th-century madrigal.

The *frottola* was aristocratic music, although popular tunes were sometimes incorporated. Under the patronage of Isabella d'Este, the *frottola* developed at the court at Mantua, and it also became popular at other courts of northern Italy, particularly at Ferrara and Urbino. Serafino dall'Aquila (d. 1500) was an important *frottola* poet. The most important composers of *frottola* were Bartolomeo Tromboncino (d. c. 1535) and Marchetto Cara (d. c. 1530). At times the same person wrote both text and music.

Frottola texts were usually of limited literary value, typically consisting of several six-line verses, each followed by a four-line refrain, using the same music.

The term *frottola* was also used for a class of compositions, some with specific poetic forms, including the *strambotto*, the *oda*, and the *barzelletta*. Ottaviano dei Petrucci, the first significant printer to use movable music type, printed 11 books of *frottole* in Venice between 1504 and 1514.

madrigals during this period. His first book of madrigals (now lost) was published in 1538 and reprinted in 1539, in which year three additional volumes of his madrigals appeared. A total of five volumes were published, and his work also appeared in anthologies of the period.

In 1540 he entered the service of Pope Paul III as choirmaster in the papal chapel in Rome. Paul died in 1549, and two years later Arcadelt moved to France. In the early 1550s he entered the service of Charles de Lorraine, 2nd cardinal de Lorraine. Apparently following the taste of his patron, after moving to France Arcadelt virtually stopped writing madrigals and concentrated instead on the writing of chansons. He is credited with having written some 126 pieces in this form. In 1557 he was choirmaster of the French royal chapel.

Arcadelt's reputation rests largely on the work he produced early in his career, his more than 200 madrigals. With two of his contemporaries, Costanzo Festa and Philippe Verdelot, Arcadelt set the style for a generation of madrigal composers. He favoured four-voiced composition, and his secular music owes much to the simple declamation and tuneful treble melody of the *frottola*, a popular Italian song genre. The simple clarity of his style influenced composers Giovanni Pierluigi da Palestrina and Cipriano de Rore. In addition to his shorter works, Arcadelt also published more than 20 motets and 3 masses.

PHILIPPE DE MONTE

(b. 1521, Mechelen, Flanders [now in Belgium]—d. July 4, 1603, Prague, Bohemia [now in Czech Republic])

Like many Netherlandish composers at the time, Philippe (also Philippus) de Monte journeyed to Italy (where he was known as Filippo di Monte) to pursue his career. He spent his early adulthood as a music instructor in the employ of a wealthy family in Naples. By 1554, the year his first book of madrigals saw publication, he had returned to the Low Countries. Monte then visited England in 1554–55 as a singer in the chapel of Philip II of Spain (the consort of Queen Mary I), and while there he befriended the adolescent William Byrd. He eventually moved back to Italy, where he lived in peripatetic fashion as a teacher and composer.

Monte was in Rome in 1568 when he became musical director to the Habsburg emperor Maximilian II at his court in Vienna. He flourished in the following years, publishing his work regularly and actively participating in prestigious royal celebrations. When Maximilian died and his son Rudolf II acceded to the throne in 1576, Monte remained in his position. Four years later he transferred to Prague, which Rudolf had made the new imperial residence. Although Monte was apparently unhappy in Rudolf's court, in which music played a less central role than it had in Maximilian's, he was highly productive. In addition, while serving the emperors, he was awarded honorary posts at Cambrai Cathedral in what is now France.

Monte's hundreds of compositions are characterized by a fluent but nonexperimental technique, and he excelled in subtle contrasts of register and voice grouping. Of the variety of voicings that appear in his repertoire, he most commonly composed for five parts. Monte's sacred works, which stand comparison with those of Italian composer Giovanni Pierluigi da Palestrina, include approximately 40 masses, most of which are parodies, and at least 250 motets that are noted for their elegance.

Although Monte wrote several dozen chansons, the overwhelming majority of his secular compositions are madrigals. Indeed, not only was he one of the last Netherlandish masters of the form, but he was the most prolific of his contemporaries, publishing more than

1,200 (including some spiritual madrigals) in nearly 40 books during his lifetime. Although Monte's madrigals are typified by their solemnity, he gradually developed an individualistic style in which balance was provided by energetic rhythms. Many of his early works in the form are settings of Petrarch.

ORLANDO DI LASSO

(b. 1530/32, Mons, Spanish Hainaut [now in Belgium]—d. June 14, 1594, Munich [Germany])

Portrait of Orlando di Lasso, a Flemish composer whose compositions earned him honours from Pope Gregory XIII and Holy Roman emperor Maximilian II. Palm/Rsch/Redferns/Getty Images

The Flemish composer known variously as Orlando di Lasso, Orlandus Lassus (Latin), or Roland de Lassus wrote music that stands at the apex of the Franco-Flemish Renaissance style. As a child he was a choirboy at St. Nicholas in Mons and because of his beautiful voice was kidnapped three times for other choirs. He was taken into the service of Ferdinand of Gonzaga, general to Charles V, and traveled with the imperial army in its French campaign in 1544. He accompanied Gonzaga to Italy in 1544, where he remained for 10 years. From 1553 to 1554 he was chapelmaster of the papal church of St. John Lateran at Rome, a post later held by Giovanni Pierluigi da Palestrina. Following a sojourn in Antwerp (1555–56), he joined the court chapel of Duke Albrecht V of Bavaria

The sheet music of a chanson, wherein Lasso had set to music a work by the French poet Pierre de Ronsard. Universal Images Group/Getty Images

in Munich, where, except for some incidental journeys, he remained for the rest of his life. In 1570 the Emperor Maximilian raised him to the nobility; and, when Lasso dedicated a collection of his masses (1574) to Pope Gregory XIII, he received the knighthood of the Golden Spur, a pontifical honour.

Of Lasso's more than 2,000 compositions, many appeared in print between 1555, when his first book of Italian madrigals was published in Venice, and 1604, when a posthumous collection of 516 Latin motets (religious choral works), *Magnum Opus Musicum*, was published by his sons. Certain volumes stand out as landmarks in his career. His first collection of motets (1556) established his mastery in a field to which he contributed all his life. A comprehensive anthology of his chansons, or French part-songs (1570), helped to consolidate his position as the leading composer in this genre. In addition to his madrigals (Italian choral pieces) and chansons, he published seven collections of lieder (German part-songs). Probably his best known work is his sombre, impressive collection of penitential Psalms, *Psalmi Davidis Poenitentiales* (1584). Its rediscovery and edition in 1838 by S.W. Dehn initiated a revival of interest in Lasso's works.

Lasso was a master in the field of sacred music and was equally at home in secular composition. In the latter field his internationalism is striking, encompassing Italian, French, and German genres. His religious works have a particular emotional intensity. He took great care to mirror the meaning of his texts in his music, a trait that looked forward to the Baroque style of the early 17th century.

GIACHES DE WERT

(b. 1535, Ghent?, Flanders [Belgium]—d. May 6, 1596, Mantua [Italy])

Flemish composer Giaches de Wert (Jaches de Vuert) was best known to his contemporaries for his madrigals. He was highly praised by contemporary musicians, particularly Giovanni Pierluigi da Palestrina, Thomas Morley, and Claudio Monteverdi. It is likely that de Wert was taken to Italy as a boy to be a singer in an aristocratic household based near Naples. About 1550 he is believed to have moved to Novellara (now in Emilia-Romagna, Italy), where he became attached to a court of the Gonzaga family. This connection may have led to his work for a few years in the early 1560s as *maestro di cappella* (choirmaster) at the governor's court in Milan. In 1565 he was appointed *maestro di cappella* to Guglielmo Gonzaga, the duke of Mantua, at the ducal chapel of Santa Barbara. He held this position until 1592, by which time his health had begun to fail.

De Wert was a prolific composer, producing a large number of both sacred and secular works of various types. Because much of his sacred music was written for the exclusive use of Santa Barbara, all but one of his seven masses and his more than 125 hymns were published after his death. Of his sacred music, only his three collections of motets were published during his lifetime. As a result, de Wert is especially recognized for his madrigals, canzonets, motets, and other occasional vocal pieces. Modern scholars have noted his influence on other composers, notably on Claudio Monteverdi, whose years at Mantua overlapped with de Wert's later tenure.

LUCA MARENZIO

(b. 1553, Coccaglio, near Brescia, Republic of Venice [now Italy]—d. Aug. 22, 1599, Rome)

Luca Marenzio, considered a master composer of madrigals, was probably trained as a choirboy in Brescia, and he was in service with Cardinal Luigi d'Este in Rome from 1578 to 1586. In 1588 he went to Florence, where he worked with the circle of musicians and poets associated with Count Giovanni Bardi. Later he was in the service of Cardinal Cinzio Aldobrandini in Rome. In 1594 he visited Sigismund III of Poland, returned to Rome in 1595, and went again to Poland in 1596. In 1598 he was in Venice and later was appointed musician at the papal court.

Marenzio published a large number of madrigals and villanelles and five books of motets. He developed an individual technique and was skilled in evoking moods and images suggested by the poetic texts of the madrigals. He exploited passages in a homophonic, or chordal, style in place of the polyphonic style characteristic of earlier madrigals. He was a daring harmonist: his chromaticism occasionally led to advanced enharmonic modulations, and he sometimes left dissonances unresolved for dramatic effect. He exerted a strong influence on Claudio Monteverdi, Don Carlo Gesualdo, and Hans Hassler and was much-admired in England, where his works were printed in N. Yonge's *Musica transalpina* (1588), a collection that stimulated the composition of English madrigals.

CARLO GESUALDO, PRINCIPE DI VENOSA, CONTE DI CONZA

(b. March 30, 1566, Venosa [Italy]—d. Sept. 8, 1613, Gesualdo)

Until the late 20th century, the reputation of Italian composer and lutenist Carlo Gesualdo rested chiefly on his dramatic, unhappy, and often bizarre life. Since the late 20th century, however, his reputation as a musician has grown, based on his highly individual and richly chromatic madrigals. He is especially noted for what music scholar

Glenn Watkins called the "dazzling harmonic style" of his last two books of madrigals.

The title of count of Conza was awarded to Gesualdo's ancestor Sansone II in 1452. The family further had received the principality of Venosa in what is now southern Italy from King Philip II of Spain in 1561, when Carlo's father, Fabrizio II, married Girolama Borromeo, the niece of Pope Pius IV. Carlo was the second-born son and was named for a maternal uncle, Carlo Borromeo, who was canonized in 1610. As the second-born son, he grew up without the cares of the primary heir, but, when his elder brother died in 1584, Carlo was expected to shoulder the responsibility for the family line and for the large estate.

In 1586 he married his first cousin, the twice-widowed Maria d'Avalos, who was several years older than he. She bore a son and not long thereafter embarked on an affair with Fabrizio Carafa, duca d'Andria. Informed of her infidelity, Gesualdo laid a trap and, with the help of others, murdered his wife and her lover in bed. The double murder caused a great scandal, and what came to be seen as a tragic outcome of the affair became the subject matter of a number of writers, including Giambattista Marino and Torquato Tasso. Because such revenge was in keeping with the social code of the day, however, Gesualdo was not charged with murder. When his father died in 1591, he assumed the title of prince of Venosa.

About two years after the demise of his first wife, the new prince of Venosa was contracted to marry Eleonora d'Este (i.e., of the house of Este) in Ferrara. Gesualdo was much interested in the widespread musical reputation of the Este court in Ferrara. In 1594 he traveled there as a composer and musician and to claim his new wife. Gesualdo likely had high expectations for this connection, but it soon became evident that he did not have the same expectations for the marriage itself; he left Ferrara without his bride a few months after the wedding and remained away for some seven months. This was a pattern of prolonged absence that he would repeat. Further, according to reports, he also abused Eleonora physically and was unfaithful to her. Yet he found the atmosphere of the Este court and his proximity to several of the leading composers of the day quite stimulating. His first two books of madrigals were published by the Ferrarese ducal press in 1594. His third book of madrigals was first published by the ducal press in 1595 and the fourth in 1596, both apparently written largely during his time in Ferrara and both showing signs of the development of his personal vision.

By early 1597 Gesualdo had again returned to his home. Reluctantly, his wife joined him in Venosa in the autumn. Early 21st-century scholarship revealed that Eleonora during the next several years initiated proceedings for witchcraft against her husband's former concubine. Testimony was given revealing that both sorcery and love potions were involved, and ultimately two women were tried and convicted. Bizarrely, the guilty parties were sentenced to imprisonment in Gesualdo's castle. The prince and his wife continued to live together intermittently, though both were unhappy and unwell for long periods at a time. In 1603 Gesualdo published two sacred motet collections.

Gesualdo's last two books of madrigals (as well as a Holy Week *Responsoria*) were published in 1611. Although these last two books of madrigals were long considered "late" works because of their dramatic exclamations, linearly driven chromaticism, discontinuous texture, and harmonic license—that is, their generally unusual and experimental nature—Gesualdo himself claimed that they had in fact been written in the mid-to-late 1590s, near the time of his other published madrigals, and that he had

RENAISSANCE MUSIC PRINTERS

Well before the end of the first century of typography, the printers had brought to the book the basic forms of nearly every element they were to contribute. The styles of the three major typefaces had been formalized to the point at which little other than refinement remained to be added to them. Most of the business and craft functions that were to mark the production of books down to the present had been identified and differentiated. The printed book had achieved an acceptance comparable to, and an audience far greater than, that of the manuscript volume. Publishing specialties had also emerged. Fully one-third of all of the books printed during the period of the incunabula—that is from the 1450s to 1500—were illustrated. The practice of numbering the pages of a volume in sequence had been adopted, and the printing of music had become practical.

A number of printers who specialized in music are still known today. One of the best known Italian printers was Ottaviano dei Petrucci (1466–1539), whose collection of chansons, *Harmonice Musices Odhecaton A* (1501), was the first polyphonic music printed from movable type. His 61 music publications contain masses, motets, chansons, and *frottole* by the foremost composers of the 15th and early 16th centuries, among them Josquin des Prez, Jean de Ockeghem, and Loyset Compère.

In France a prominent Renaissance music printer and publisher was Pierre Attaingnant (Attaignant; c. 1494–1551/52). He was one of the earliest to use single-impression printing. (Earlier printers had printed the staff and the notes in separate impressions.) Before 1527 Attaingnant began using a newly invented movable music type, in which a fragment of a musical staff was combined with a note on each piece of type. He used the new type in a book of chansons, *Chansons Nouvelles* (1528). Because Attaingnant's single-impression method halved the time and labour formerly needed to print music, it was quickly adopted throughout Europe. Attaingnant was the first to use the printing press to achieve mass production in music publishing. Attaingnant's printings represent more than 150 outstanding composers of his day. His 111 surviving publications are rich in information about early 16th-century music.

The Ballard family, also of France, virtually monopolized music printing there from 1560 to 1750. The founder of the dynasty was Robert Ballard (d. 1588), brother-in-law to the celebrated lutenist and composer Adrian Le Roy. These two used movable type, cut in 1540 by Robert's father-in-law, Guillaume Le Bé (or du Gué). Their first patent was granted in 1552 as sole music printers to Henry II. With the provision of further patents, the business continued in the family until 1788. It may be noted that the women of the Ballard family were often as active in the business as the men. Ballard publications, both those with the early movable type and the later ones engraved on copper plates, were noted for their beauty and care of presentation. Their title pages were frequently superb examples of decorative engraving. The music published represented practically all the French composers of the period, among them Clément Janequin, Claude Goudimel, and Orlando di Lasso.

English publisher Thomas East (Easte, Est, or Este; c. 1540–1609) was especially noteworthy for his collection of Psalms (1592), which was one of the first instances of part-music printed in score rather than as individual parts in separate books. East became an assignee in the music-publishing monopoly granted by Elizabeth I to the composers William Byrd and Thomas Tallis. His first publication was Byrd's *Psalmes, Sonets and Songs of Sadnes and Pietie* (1588). In 1592 he edited *The Whole Booke of Psalmes, With Their Wonted Tunes*, harmonizations of psalm tunes by prominent musicians. His madrigal books included collections by Thomas Weelkes, John Wilbye, and Thomas Morley.

been forced to publish accurate copies because inaccurate copies had been printed and some work plagiarized.

GIOVANNI PIERLUIGI DA PALESTRINA

(b. c. 1525, Palestrina, near Rome—d. Feb. 2, 1594, Rome)

Italian composer Giovanni Pierluigi da Palestrina, a master of contrapuntal composition, wrote more than 105 masses and 250 motets. Living during the period of the Catholic Counter-Reformation, Palestrina was a primary representative of the 16th-century conservative approach to church music.

LIFE

Palestrina was born in a small town where his ancestors are thought to have lived for generations, but as a child he was taken to nearby Rome. In 1537 he was one of the choirboys at the basilica of Santa Maria Maggiore, where he also studied music between 1537 and 1539. In 1544 Palestrina was engaged as organist and singer in the cathedral of his native town. His duties included playing the organ, helping with the choir, and teaching music. His pay was that of a canon and would have been received in money and kind. His prowess at the church there attracted the attention of the bishop, Giovanni Maria Ciocchi del Monte, who later became Pope Julius III.

In 1547 Palestrina married Lucrezia Gori. Three sons were born to them: Rodolfo, Angelo, and Iginio. Only the last outlived his father. In 1551 Palestrina returned to Rome, where he assumed the first of his papal appointments, as musical director of the Julian Chapel choir, and thus was responsible for the music in St. Peter's. Before he was 30 he published his first book of masses (1554), dedicated to Julius III, and the following year he was

Portrait of Giovanni Pierluigi da Palestrina, whose patrons included Pope Julius III. © The Art Archive/SuperStock

promoted to singer in the Pontifical Choir. About this
time he became composer to the papal chapel. Palestrina
repaid the Pope's patronage by composing a mass in his
honour. Yet he did not neglect the secular side of his art,
for his first book of madrigals (secular and spiritual part-
songs) appeared in 1555, unfortunately at a time when the
lenient regime of Julius III had given way to the sterner
discipline of Paul IV. A decree of the new pope forbade
married men to serve in the papal choir, and Palestrina,
together with two of his colleagues, received a small pension by way of compensation for their dismissal.

For the next five years Palestrina directed the choir of
St. John Lateran, but his efforts were continually thwarted
by singers whose quality was almost as limited as their
number, which was restricted because very little money
was available for music. Nevertheless, he gained admission
for his eldest son, Rodolfo, then about 13, as a chorister.
Eventually he broke away from this uncongenial milieu.
The chapter archives of St. John Lateran record that in
July 1560 he and his son suddenly departed.

A year passed before Palestrina found employment. In
March 1561 he accepted a new post at Sta. Maria Maggiore.
This post was more congenial to him and he remained
at it for about seven years. At the invitation of Cardinal
Ippolito d'Este he then took charge of the music at the
Villa d'Este in Tivoli, a popular summer resort near Rome.
He was in the Cardinal's service for four years, at which
time he also worked as music master for a newly formed
Seminarium Romanum (Roman Seminary), where his sons
Rodolfo and Angelo became students.

Palestrina received an offer in 1568 to become musical director at the court of the emperor Maximilian II in
Vienna. He refused the position because of the low salary
and a disinclination to leave Rome. Palestrina's terms were
also too high when he was invited to the court at Mantua

in 1583. The composer and the duke of Mantua, Guglielmo Gonzaga, an amateur musician of some pretensions, did become friends, however, and Palestrina was commissioned to write special compositions for the ducal chapel of Sta. Barbara.

With the death in 1571 of the composer Giovanni Animuccia, musical director at the Vatican since 1555, there was a chance for Palestrina to return to his old post as musical director of the Julian choir. The chapter, eager to have him back, increased the salary, and he forthwith returned to St. Peter's. When his growing fame as a composer prompted Sta. Maria Maggiore to rehire him, St. Peter's again raised his salary. In acknowledgment of his position as the most celebrated Roman musician, he was given in 1578 the title of master of music at the Vatican Basilica.

The series of epidemics that swept through central Italy in the late 1570s carried off his wife and his two elder sons, both of whom showed great musical promise. He himself fell seriously ill. Grieving over his wife's death, he announced his intention of becoming a priest, to the delight of the pope, Gregory XIII. After having been made a canon, however, he renounced his vows in order to marry (1581) Virginia Dormoli, widow of a wealthy merchant. Although he spent considerable time administering her fortune, he retained his position at St. Peter's and continued to compose.

Although an attempt in 1585 to make Palestrina musical director of the Pontifical Choir proved abortive, he was considered by all the popes under whom he served as the official composer for the choir, and it is recorded that he marched at the head of the pontifical singers on the occasion of erecting the great Egyptian obelisk in the piazza of St. Peter's.

Pope Gregory XIII had commissioned Palestrina and Annibale Zoilo to restore the plainchant, or plainsong (a traditional liturgical chant sung in unison), then in use to a more authentic form. The task proved too great, and Palestrina's editorial work gave way to a flow of creative music. Much of it was published during the last 12 years of his life, including volumes of motets (choral compositions based on sacred texts), masses, and madrigals. He also helped to found an association of professional musicians called the Vertuosa Compagnia dei Musici.

Two years before Palestrina's death, the new pope, Clement VIII, increased his pension, and the same year, in a singular mark of respect and admiration, fellow composers paid their elderly senior the compliment of writing 16 settings of the Vesper Psalms to his praise. In return, Palestrina sent them a motet on the appropriate text: *Vos amici mei estis* ("You are my friends, if you do what I teach, said the Lord").

MUSIC

Palestrina's musical output, though vast, maintained a remarkably high standard in both sacred and secular works. His 105 masses embrace many different styles, and the number of voices used ranges from four to eight. The time-honoured technique of using a cantus firmus (preexistent melody used in one voice part) as the tenor is found in such masses as *Ecce sacerdos magnus*; *L'Homme armé*; *Ut, re, mi, fa, sol, la*; *Ave Maria*; *Tu es Petrus*; and *Veni Creator Spiritus*. These titles refer to the source of the particular cantus firmus. Palestrina's mastery of contrapuntal ingenuity may be appreciated to the fullest extent in some of his canonic masses (in which one or more voice parts are derived from another voice part). His ability to ornament and decorate a solemn plainchant, making it an integral part of the texture and sometimes almost indistinguishable from the other, freely composed parts, is evident from some of his masses based on hymn melodies.

By far the greatest number of masses employ what has come to be known as the parody technique, by which a composer made use either of his own music or that of others as a starting point for the new composition. Many other masses derive from musical ideas by Palestrina's predecessors or contemporaries. Yet another type of mass is demonstrated by the nine works written for Mantua; in these the Gloria and Credo sections are so arranged that plainsong and polyphony alternate throughout. Finally, there is a small but important group of masses that are in free style, the musical material being entirely original. Perhaps the best known example is the *Missa brevis* for four voices.

Palestrina's motets, of which more than 250 are extant, display almost as much variety of form and type as do his masses. Most of them are in some clearly defined form, occasionally reflecting the shape of the liturgical text, though comparatively few are based on plainsong. Many of them paraphrase the chant, however, with an artistry that is every bit as successful as that of the masses. On the same level as the canonic masses are such motets as *Cum ortus fuerit* and *Accepit Jesus calicem*, the latter apparently a favourite of the composer's—an assumption justified because he is depicted holding a copy of it in a portrait now in the Vatican.

His 29 motets based on texts from the Song of Solomon afford numerous examples of "madrigalisms": the use of suggestive musical phrases evoking picturesque features, apparent either to the ear or to the eye, sometimes to both. In the offertories, Palestrina completely abandons the old cantus firmus technique and writes music in free style, whereas in the hymns he paraphrases the traditional melody, usually in the highest voice. In the *Lamentations of Jeremiah* he brings effective contrast to bear on the sections with Hebrew and Latin text, the former being melismatic (floridly vocalized) in style and the latter simpler and more solemn. His Magnificats are mainly in four sets of eight, each set comprising a Magnificat on one of the eight "tones": *alternatim* structure is used here as in the Mantua masses.

Although Palestrina's madrigals are generally considered of less interest than his sacred music, they show as keen a sense for pictorial and pastoral elements as one finds in any of his contemporaries. Over and above this, he is to be remembered for his early exploitation of the narrative sonnet in madrigal form, notably in *Vestiva i colli*, which was frequently reprinted and imitated. His settings of Petrarch's poems also are of an exceptionally high order.

At the end of the 19th century the view that Palestrina represented the loftiest peak of Italian polyphony was in some ways detrimental to his reputation, for it cast his music into rigid preconceptions. Even more unfortunate was the insistence on "counterpoint in the style of Palestrina" in the examination requirements of academies and universities, for such requirements stultified a style that Palestrina had used with great flexibility. Generations of fledgling composers were taught to revere the music of Palestrina as a symbol of all that was pure in ecclesiastical counterpoint. Indeed, the greater part of his musical output, and in particular his masses (where his unerring sense of tonal architecture may be heard at its best), still remains worthy of admiration.

Palestrina, unlike Johann Sebastian Bach, did not have to be rediscovered in the 19th century, though the dissemination of his achievement was helped by the interest of Romantic composers. There always was a Palestrinian tradition, mainly because his music supplied the need for a well-regulated formal system to be used by the embryonic composer in presenting himself to the musical world. Strict counterpoint was associated with a technique acquired in this way. In his day, Palestrina was a senior figure who, utilizing the dominant style of his time, created works notable for their spiritual qualities and technical mastery.

ANDREA GABRIELI

(b. 1532/33, Venice—d. Aug. 30, 1585, Venice)

Italian composer and organist Andrea Gabrieli is known for his madrigals and his large-scale choral and instrumental music for public ceremonies. His finest work was composed for the acoustic resources of the Cathedral of St. Mark in Venice. He was the uncle of Giovanni Gabrieli. (He is also called Andrea di Cannaregio [Cannaregio is a district of Venice]).

In the late 1550s Gabrieli left Italy for an extended period of foreign travel. He served in the Bavarian court chapel at Munich under another great Franco-Fleming, Orlando di Lasso, then visited the court of Graz in Austria, and finally was patronized by the noble Fugger family in Augsburg. In 1564 he returned to Venice to become second organist at St. Mark's, where he remained until 1584, when he succeeded the virtuoso performer Claudio Merulo as first organist—a position he held until his death in 1586. Despite his profession, not much of his output in these years was organ music; there were several volumes of madrigals, settings of Italian poetry to be sung at private houses or cultural academies, where musical life flourished. He also contributed large-scale choral and instrumental music for ceremonies of church and state, the music for which he is best-known today. His motets and masses exploit the tonal variety possible when instruments are added to a choir. Some of these works were published posthumously in 1587: one of the finest is the *Magnificat* for three choirs and orchestra, doubtless intended to be performed in St. Mark's.

GIOVANNI GABRIELI

(b. 1556?, Venice [Italy]—d. Aug. 12?, 1612, Venice)

Italian composer, organist, and teacher Giovanni Gabrieli is celebrated for his sacred music, including massive choral and instrumental motets for the liturgy. He studied with his uncle, Andrea Gabrieli, whom he regarded with almost filial affection. His uncle's foreign travels and connections gave Giovanni, who traveled with him, the opportunity to become known abroad. Giovanni also served (1575–79) under Orlando di Lasso in Munich. In 1584 he returned to Venice and a year later succeeded his uncle as second organist of St. Mark's Cathedral—the post he held for life.

After Andrea's death in 1585, Giovanni quickly assumed the limelight in the field of ceremonial music, though he was never so active as a madrigalist. The publication of his uncle's music in 1587 was a mark of respect but also included some of his own church music. Giovanni's foreign connections included Hans Leo Hassler, the German composer and former pupil of Andrea, who avidly adopted the Venetian style, and patrons such as the Fugger family and Archduke Ferdinand of Austria. In later years Giovanni became a famous teacher. His most notable student was the German Heinrich Schütz.

After 1587 Giovanni's principal publications were the two immense *Sacrae symphoniae* of 1597 and 1615 (printed posthumously), both of which contained purely instrumental music for church use or massive choral and instrumental motets for the liturgy. Like his uncle, he usually conceived the music for separated choirs but showed an increasing tendency to specify which instruments were to be used and which choirs were to consist of soloists and full choir, as well as to distinguish the musical style of each, thus initiating a completely new approach to the creation of musical colour and orchestration. In the well-known *Sonata pian e forte*, for eight instruments, directions to play loud and soft are given. Among the motets, his masterpiece is perhaps *In ecclesiis*, for four soloists, four-part choir, violin, three cornets, two trombones, and organ, these forces pitted against one another in an endless variety of combinations.

CLAUDIO MONTEVERDI

(baptized May 15, 1567, Cremona, Duchy of Milan [Italy]—d. Nov. 29, 1643, Venice)

Italian composer Claudio Monteverdi was the most important developer of the then-new genre, the opera. He studied with the director of music at Cremona Cathedral, Marcantonio Ingegneri, a well-known musician who wrote church music and madrigals of some distinction in an up-to-date though not revolutionary style of the 1570s. Monteverdi was obviously a precocious pupil, since he published several books of religious and secular music in his teens, all of them containing competent pieces in a manner not far from that of his master. The culmination of this early period occurred in two madrigal books published by one of the most famous of Venetian printers in 1587 and 1590. They are full of excellent, attractive works, somewhat more modern in approach than Ingegneri's, perhaps the result of studying the madrigals of Luca Marenzio (1553–99), the greatest Italian madrigalist of the time, and others. As yet, however, Monteverdi's aim appeared to be to charm rather than to express passion. It is exemplified

Colour sketch of Claudio Monteverdi, the Italian composer who was instrumental in shaping the musical and dramatic conventions of opera. DEA/A. Dagli Orti/De Agostini/Getty Images

at its best in such a madrigal as the well-known setting of the poem "Behold the Murmuring Sea" by Torquato Tasso.

THE GONZAGA COURT

It is not known exactly when Monteverdi left his hometown, but he entered the employ of the duke of Mantua about 1590 as a string player. He immediately came into contact with some of the finest musicians, both performers and composers, of the time. Most influential on him seems to have been the Flemish composer Giaches de Wert, a modernist who, although no longer a young man, was still in the middle of an avant-garde movement in the 1590s. The crux of his style was that music must exactly match the mood of the verse and that the natural declamation of the words must be carefully followed. Since he chose the highly concentrated, emotional lyric poetry of Tasso and Tasso's rival Battista Guarini, Wert's music also became highly emotional, if unmelodious and difficult to sing. It had an immediate effect on Monteverdi, whose next book of madrigals, published in his first year at Mantua, shows the influence of the new movement on him, though his understanding was imperfect. It represented a complete change of direction for him. The melody is angular, the harmony increasingly dissonant, the mood tense to the point of neurosis. Guarini is the favoured poet, and every nuance of the verse is expressed, even at the expense of musical balance.

The new style and ambience seems to have upset his productivity. Although he went on composing, he published little for the next 11 years. In 1595 he accompanied his employer on an expedition to Hungary and four years later to Flanders. In about 1599 he married a singer, Claudia Cattaneo, by whom he had three children, one of whom died in infancy. When the post of *maestro di cappella*, or director of music, to the duke became vacant on the death of Wert in 1596, Monteverdi was embittered at being passed over, but in 1602 he achieved the position, at the age of 35. He published two more books of madrigals in 1603 and 1605, both of which contain masterpieces. The avant-garde manner was now better assimilated into his idiom. While his aim was still to follow the meaning of the verse in great detail, he solved the purely musical problems of thematic development and proportion. Although the dissonances became more severe and the melody sometimes still more angular, the total effect was more varied in emotion and less neurotic. If Guarini's eroticism stimulated a sensual musical style, Monteverdi often gave his mature madrigals a lightness and humour, seeing the essence of a poem rather than its detail.

It was the advanced musical means, especially the use of intense and prolonged dissonance, that provoked attacks by the conservatives on Monteverdi, who became a figurehead of the avant-garde group. The attacks by a Bolognese theorist, Giovanni Maria Artusi, in a series of pamphlets, made Monteverdi the most famous composer of the age and provoked him to reply with an important aesthetic statement of his view on the nature of his art. He disclaimed the role of revolutionary, saying that he was only the follower of a tradition that had been developing for the last 50 years or more. This tradition sought to create a union of the arts, especially of words and music, so that he should not be judged simply as a composer using conventional musical devices. Moreover, the artwork must be powerful enough to "move the whole man," and this again might mean the abandonment of certain conventions. On the other hand, he declared his faith in another and older tradition, in which music was itself supreme, and which was, in effect, represented by the pure polyphony of such composers as Josquin des Prez and Palestrina. Thus, there were two "practices," as he called them. This view, which became immensely influential, was to prove the basis of the preservation of an old style in certain types of church music, as opposed to a modern style in opera and cantatas, a dichotomy that can be found well into the 19th century.

If the madrigals of this time gave him a reputation well outside northern Italy, it was his first opera, *Orfeo*, performed in 1607, that finally established him as a composer of large-scale music rather than of exquisite miniature works. Monteverdi may have attended some of the performances of the earliest operas, those composed by the Florentine composers Jacopo Peri and Giulio Caccini, and he certainly had written some stage music in previous years. In *Orfeo* he showed that he had a much broader conception of the new genre than did his predecessors. He combined the opulence of dramatic entertainments of the late Renaissance with the straightforwardness of a simple pastoral tale told in recitative, which was the ideal of the Florentines. His recitative is more flexible and expressive than theirs, based on the declamatory melody of his madrigals rather than on their theories about heightened speech. Above all, he had a greater gift for dramatic unity, shaping whole acts into musical units, rather than assembling them from small sections. He also showed a sense of matching the climaxes in the drama by musical climaxes, using dissonance, the singer's virtuosity, or instrumental sonorities to create the sense of heightened emotion.

A few months after the production of *Orfeo*, Monteverdi suffered the loss of his wife, seemingly after a long illness. He retired in a state of deep depression to his father's home at Cremona, but he was summoned back to Mantua almost immediately to compose a new opera as part of the celebrations on the occasion of the marriage of the heir to the duchy, Francesco Gonzaga, to Margaret of Savoy. Monteverdi returned unwillingly and was promptly submerged in a massive amount of work. He composed not only an opera but also a ballet and music for an intermezzo to a play. Further disaster occurred when the opera, *L'Arianna*, was in rehearsal, for the prima donna, a young girl who had been living in Monteverdi's home, possibly as a pupil of his wife, died of smallpox. Nevertheless, the part was recast, and the opera was finally produced in May 1608. It was an enormous success. The score has been lost, except for the famous "Lamento," which survives in various versions and is the first great operatic *scena* (i.e., a scene of especially dramatic effect, usually with arias).

After this enormous effort, Monteverdi returned again to Cremona in a condition of collapse, which seems to have lasted for a long time. He was ordered back to Mantua in November 1608 but refused to go. He eventually returned, but thereafter he hated the Gonzaga court, which he maintained had undervalued and underpaid him, though he gained a raise in pay and a small pension for his success with *L'Arianna*. He does not, however, appear to have been uncreative, though the music he wrote in the next year or so reflects his depression. He arranged the "Lamento" as a five-voiced madrigal and wrote a madrigalian threnody on the death of his prima donna. The sestina, published later in the sixth book of madrigals, represents the peak of dissonant, agonized music in this style. In a more vigorous vein, he wrote some church music, which he published in 1610 in a volume containing a mass in the old style and music for vespers on feasts of the Blessed Virgin Mary. The mass was a remarkable achievement, a deliberate attempt to show that the polyphonic idiom was still possible when everywhere it was dying. Still more remarkable is the vespers music, a virtual compendium of all the kinds of modern church music possible at the time—grand psalm settings in the Venetian manner, virtuoso music for solo singers, instrumental music used for interludes in the service, even an attempt to use up-to-date operatic music to set the expressive, emotional words of the Magnificat. Yet, though this music is as "advanced" as possible, Monteverdi makes it an extension of the old tradition by using plainsong tunes—ancient unaccompanied liturgical chants—as the thematic material for the Psalms and Magnificats. Above all, this is music of the Counter-Reformation. Using all means, traditional and new, secular and religious, it is designed to impress the listener with the power of the Roman Catholic Church and its Maker.

THREE DECADES IN VENICE

When the *maestro di cappella*—that is, the director of music—of St. Mark's in Venice died, Monteverdi was invited to take his place, after an audition of some of his music in the basilica. He finally took up his appointment in the autumn of 1613.

He was appointed largely because the musical establishment of St. Mark's was in need of an experienced director after some years of decline. The last of the native Venetian composers of any distinction, Giovanni Gabrieli, had recently died. Although Monteverdi had not been primarily a church musician, he took his duties extremely seriously and within a few years completely revitalized the music in the basilica. He hired new assistants (including two future composers of note, Francesco Cavalli and Alessandro Grandi), wrote much church music, and insisted on daily choral services. He also took an active part in music making elsewhere in the city, directing the music on several occasions for the fraternity of S. Rocco, an influential philanthropic brotherhood, on the annual festival of its patron saint.

His letters in those early years in Venice reveal a complete change in his state of mind from what it was in Mantua. He felt fulfilled and honoured, well (and regularly) paid, and he seems to have been reasonably prolific. He kept up his links with Mantua, largely because there was little chance of producing opera in Venice, while opportunities came quite regularly from the Gonzaga court. In his correspondence, a philosophy of dramatic music emerges that was not only to mold Monteverdi's later work but also to influence the history of opera in general. The older type of opera had developed, on the one hand, from the Renaissance intermezzo—a short, static musical treatment, often allegorical and with scenery, of a subject from the play with which it was given, emphasizing the wishes of the gods; and, on the other hand, from the pastoral, with its highly artificial characterizations of shepherds and shepherdesses. Monteverdi, however, was increasingly concerned with the expression of human emotions and the creation of recognizable human beings, with their changes of mind and mood. Thus, he wished to develop a greater variety of musical means, and in his seventh book of madrigals (1619) he experimented with many new devices. Most were borrowed from the current practices of his younger contemporaries, but all were endowed with greater power. There are the conversational "musical letters," deliberately written in a severe recitative melody in an attempt to match the words. The ballet *Tirsi e Clori*, written for Mantua in 1616, shows, on the contrary, a complete acceptance of the simple tunefulness of the modern aria.

His attempt to create a practical philosophy of music went on throughout the 1620s, leading to still further stylistic innovations. Following ideas derived from Plato, he divided the emotions into three basic kinds: those of love, war, and calmness. Each of these could be expressed by differing rhythms and harmonies. A further ingredient in his theories was a frank acceptance of realism—the imitating of the sounds of nature in various ways. All these ideas are to be found in his dramatic cantata, *The Combat of Tancredi and Clorinda* (1624), a setting of a section of Tasso's "Gerusalemme Liberata." In this work, the rapid reiteration of single notes in strict rhythms and the use of pizzicato—plucking strings—to express the clashing of swords show important steps forward in the idiomatic use of stringed instruments.

These trends were continued in a comic opera, *Licoris Who Feigned Madness*, probably intended for the celebrations of the accession of Duke Vincenzo II of Mantua in 1627. The score has been lost, but a sizable correspondence survives. At this time, Monteverdi suffered more anxiety since his elder son, Massimiliano, was imprisoned in Bologna, where he was a medical student, for reading books banned by the Inquisition. It took some months before he was finally cleared of the charge. In the same year, 1628, Monteverdi also fulfilled a commission to write music for the intermezzi to Tasso's *L'Aminta* and for a tournament given in Parma in celebration of the marriage of Duke Odoardo Farnese to Margherita de' Medici.

Monteverdi and his family seemed to have emerged unscathed from the plague that broke out in 1630, and Monteverdi himself took holy orders during this period. He wrote a grand mass for the thanksgiving service in St. Mark's when the epidemic was officially declared over in November 1631. The "Gloria" from it still survives and shows him applying some of the theories concerning the diversity of mood suggested by the words. Both this and some other church music probably written about this time, however, show a calm and majestic approach rather than the passion of his earlier years. A book of lighthearted songs and duets published in the following year is much

Scene from a 1975 San Francisco Opera production of Claudio Monteverdi's The Coronation of Poppea. *One of the few extant operatic scores penned by Monteverdi,* Poppea *is considered a masterpiece.* Ron Scherl/Redferns/Getty Images

the same. There is also a detached quality about much of the music in the final collection of his madrigals assembled by Monteverdi himself in 1638. A vast retrospective anthology of music dating from 1608 onward, it sets out to display Monteverdi's theories, as its title, *Madrigals of War and Love*, denotes.

Though this collection, put together when Monteverdi was more than 70 years old, might seem the end of his career, chance played a part in inspiring him to an Indian summer of astonishing productivity: the first public opera houses opened in Venice in 1637. As the one indigenous composer with any real experience in the genre, he naturally was involved with them almost from the beginning.

L'Arianna was revived again, and no fewer than four new operas were composed within about three years. Only two of them have survived in score—*The Return of Ulysses to His Country* and *The Coronation of Poppea*—and both are masterpieces. Although they still retain some elements of the Renaissance intermezzo and pastoral, they can be fairly described as the first modern operas. Their interest lies in revealing the development of human beings in realistic situations. There are main plots and subplots, allowing for a great range of characters—the nobility, their servants, the evil, the misguided, the innocent, the good. The music expresses their emotions with astonishing accuracy. Monteverdi shows how the philosophy of music evolved during his early years in Venice could be put to use, using all the means available to a composer of the time, the fashionable arietta (i.e., a short aria), duets, and ensembles, and how they could be combined with the expressive and less fashionable recitative of the early part of the century. The emphasis is always on the drama: the musical units are rarely self-contained but are usually woven into a continual pattern so that the music remains a means rather than an end. There is also a sense of looking toward the grand climax of the drama, which inspires a grand *scena* for one of the main singers, Ulisse, Nero, or Poppea. At the same time, there are enough memorable melodies for the opera to seem musically attractive.

With these works Monteverdi proved himself to be one of the greatest musical dramatists of all time. That he was held in the highest esteem by his Venetian employers is shown by their gifts of money in these last years and by their granting him leave to travel to his native city in the last few months of his life. The Venetian public showed its esteem at his funeral, when after his death following a short illness, he was buried in the Church of the Frari, where a monument to him remains.

CHAPTER 5

LATER RENAISSANCE COMPOSERS ACTIVE IN ENGLAND

Another centre of musical activity was England. It, too, had its great patrons of the arts, including the Tudors and Stuarts, and the Elizabethan period in particular was enormously creative.

ROBERT FAYRFAX

(b. April 23, 1464, Deeping Gate, Lincolnshire, Eng.—d. Oct. 24, 1521, St. Albans, Hertfordshire)

Robert Fayrfax was foremost among the early English Tudor composers, noted principally for his masses and motets written in a style less florid than that of his predecessors. He is distinguished from his English contemporaries by his more frequent use of imitative counterpoint and the freedom with which he varies the number of voices employed during the course of a single composition.

Nothing is known of his career until 1497, when he was granted the first of a series of benefices as reward for his services as singer and composer. He is referred to as one of the gentlemen of the King's Chapel, a position he held until the year of his death. He received his greatest honour in 1520, when he was put in charge of the Chapel Royal musicians when they accompanied Henry VIII to his meeting with Francis I of France at the Field of Cloth of Gold.

Fayrfax was twice awarded the degree of doctor of music, at Cambridge in 1504 and at Oxford (where his degree is the earliest such known) in 1511. The mass *O quam glorifica*, composed for his Cambridge doctorate, is one of five complete extant masses, all for five voices and based on devotional verses. His surviving work also includes excellent examples of secular music, including instrumental arrangements of jigs and hornpipes.

JOHN TAVERNER

(b. c. 1490, South Lincolnshire, Eng.—d. Oct. 15, 1545, Boston, Lincolnshire)

John Taverner is known primarily for his sacred works. His music represents the culmination of early 16th-century English polyphony.

In 1526 Taverner went to the University of Oxford to become master of the choir in the chapel of Cardinal College (later Christ Church). He left Oxford in 1530 to serve as a lay clerk in St. Boltoph choir in Boston, England, where he may have taken up the position of chorister instructor. However, by 1537 he had ended his association with the choir, at which time he may have retired from employment in church music altogether. The allegation that

Drawing of John Taverner, who probably wrote all of his church music while directing choirs at Oxford University and in his hometown of Boston, England. Universal Images Group/Getty Images

he served as a paid agent of Thomas Cromwell in Henry VIII's suppression of English monasteries cannot be verified.

Taverner's church music, which is printed in *Tudor Church Music*, volumes 1 and 3 (1923–24), shows a variety, skill, range, and power that represent the climax of pre-Reformation English music. It includes 8 masses (e.g., *The Western Wind*), a few mass movements, 3 Magnificats, a Te Deum, and 28 motets. Taverner's adaptation of the musical setting of the words *In nomine Domini* from the Benedictus of his mass *Gloria tibi Trinitas* became the prototype for a large number of instrumental compositions known as In nomines, or *Gloria tibi Trinitas*.

CHRISTOPHER TYE

(b. c. 1505, Eng.—d. 1572/73)

Composer, poet, and organist Christopher Tye was an innovator in the style of English cathedral music later perfected by Thomas Tallis, William Byrd, and Orlando Gibbons.

Very little is known of Tye's early life, but the first verifiable documentation states that he earned a bachelor of music degree in 1536, that he had studied music for some 10 years, and that he had extensive experience in composing and teaching. He became a lay clerk in 1537, and about 1541 he took the position of choirmaster and organist of Ely Cathedral. He went on to receive the doctor of music degree in 1545 from King's College, Cambridge, and three years later received a doctoral degree in music at the University of Oxford. There is strong evidence that Tye served in some capacity in the royal court, possibly as music tutor to the young Edward VI and probably thanks to the influence of Richard Cox. In 1553 he published his only volume of verse and musical settings, *The Actes of the Apostles*, which were simple hymnlike compositions written for domestic use. He was ordained first as a deacon and then as a priest in 1560, and he ended his probably intermittent position as Ely's choirmaster the following year. After retiring from Ely, he held several livings as a priest. Although there is no official record of his death, a successor was appointed to one of his benefices on March 15, 1573.

Tye, like Tallis, bridged the mid-16th-century change of musical style and of liturgy (from Roman to Anglican) in England. Much of his Latin church music is incomplete, but three masses survive. His surviving Latin music has a progressive feel, with the introduction of Continental characteristics such as lively rhythms, duple time, and shorter melismas. His other surviving works include more than a dozen English anthems, at least one Magnificat, a Te Deum, several motets, psalm settings, and pieces of music for instrumental ensembles, including several works based on the plainsong fragment In nomine. His English works were especially influential in establishing a style for music in the Reformed church during the reign of Edward VI, who commanded that choirs sing in English with one note to every syllable.

THOMAS TALLIS

(b. c. 1510 — d. Nov. 23, 1585, Greenwich, London)

Thomas Tallis is one of the most important English composers of sacred music before William Byrd. His style encompassed the simple Reformation service music and the great Continental polyphonic schools whose influence he was largely responsible for introducing into English music.

Nothing is known of Tallis's education. In 1532 he held a post at Dover Priory and in 1537 at St. Mary-at-Hill,

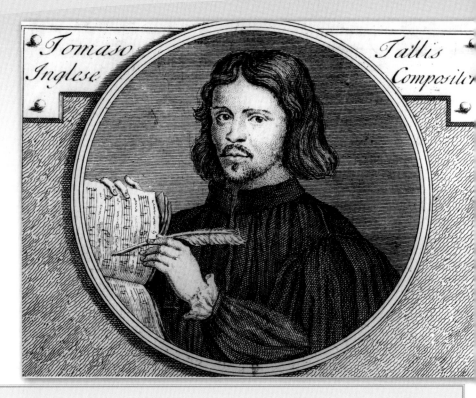

Portrait of Thomas Tallis, who, in 1575, was one of two composers (along with William Byrd) granted a monopoly on printing music and music paper in England by Queen Elizabeth I. Hulton Archive/Getty Images

London. His name appears in a list of persons who in 1540 received wages and rewards for services at the dissolution of Waltham Abbey in Essex. From Waltham he appears to have gone briefly to Canterbury and then to the Chapel Royal. In a petition to Queen Elizabeth I, made jointly with William Byrd in 1577, he refers to having "served your Majestie and your Royall ancestors these fortie years," but his appointment as a gentleman of the Chapel Royal can hardly have been before 1542.

On Jan. 21, 1575, Queen Elizabeth granted Tallis and Byrd the monopoly for printing music and music paper in England. The first publication under their license was

FITZWILLIAM VIRGINAL BOOK

The *Fitzwilliam Virginal Book* is an early 17th-century English manuscript collection of 297 pieces for keyboard by many of the major composers of the period, including William Byrd, who is represented by 67 pieces; John Bull (44); Giles Farnaby (52); and Peter Philips (19). In his preface to the 1899 edition, W. Barclay Squire proposed that the original manuscript had been copied by the younger Francis Tregian (1574?–1618) during a long confinement for recusancy in the Fleet Prison in London. This speculation has since been discounted in several respects, from the duration of his stay in prison to the reason for his confinement there (debt, rather than religious beliefs). It seems certain that the collection was the product of scholarly care and the love of music intended to record and collate popular and well-written music for the virginal. The manuscript, which bears the collector's initials and various abbreviations of his name, was acquired by Richard, 7th Viscount Fitzwilliam of Merrion, and together with the remainder of his music library and his art and medieval manuscript collections, it forms the core of the collections at the Fitzwilliam Museum, Cambridge, England. The *Fitzwilliam Virginal Book* was published in 1894–99.

a collection of 34 motets, 16 by Tallis and 18 by Byrd, entitled *Cantiones sacrae*, printed by T. Vautrollier in 1575. These Latin pieces, together with five anthems to English texts printed by John Day in his *Certaine Notes...* (1560–65), comprise all of his music that Tallis saw in print during his lifetime.

Tallis's Latin works include a modest, unnamed four-part mass; a five-part mass, *Salve intemerata*, derived from his antiphon of the same name; a seven-part mass; and two settings of the Magnificat. He also made two settings of the Lamentations of Jeremiah, the first of which is among his most celebrated works. Finally, among his Latin pieces two in particular are often cited as demonstrations of Tallis's supreme mastery of the art of counterpoint: the seven-part *Miserere nostri*, an extraordinary feat of canonic writing, involving retrograde movement together with several degrees of augmentation; and the famous 40-part *Spem in alium*, considered a unique monument in British music.

Tallis was one of the first composers to provide settings of the English liturgy. He has left settings of the Preces and Responses, the Litany, and a complete Service "in the Dorian mode," which consists of the morning and evening canticles and the Communion Service. There are also three sets of Psalms, and a number of anthems.

Tallis's keyboard music is regarded as substantial and significant. Of his 23 extant keyboard pieces, 18 occur in the mid-16th-century manuscript known as the *Mulliner Book*.

WILLIAM BYRD

(b. 1539/40, London, Eng. — d. July 4, 1623, Stondon Massey, Essex, Eng.)

English organist and composer William Byrd is best known for his development of the English madrigal. He also wrote virginal and organ music that elevated the English keyboard style.

LIFE

Of Byrd's origins and early life in London little is known. He was a pupil and protégé of the organist and composer

Thomas Tallis, and his first authenticated appointment was as organist at Lincoln Cathedral (1563). In 1572 he returned to London to take up his post as a gentleman of the Chapel Royal, where he shared the duties of organist with Tallis.

The close personal and professional relationship between the two men had important musical consequences. In 1575 Elizabeth I granted them a joint monopoly for the importing, printing, publishing, and sale of music and the printing of music paper. The first work under their imprint appeared in that year—a collection of *Cantiones sacrae* dedicated to the queen. Of the 34 motets, Tallis contributed 16 and Byrd 18.

Portrait of British composer William Byrd, noted primarily for madrigals and keyboard compositions that elevated the status of those particular musical styles in England. Hulton Archive/Getty Images

In 1577 Byrd and his family moved to Harlington, Middlesex. As a devout lifelong Roman Catholic, he probably preferred the greater privacy of living outside London. Yet, in spite of his close social contact with many other Catholics, some of whom were certainly implicated in treasonable activities, his own loyalty to the government was never questioned.

The death of Tallis in 1585 may have prompted Byrd to set his musical house in order, for in the next three years he published four collections of his own music: *Psalmes, Sonets, & Songs of Sadnes and Pietie* (1588), *Songs of Sundrie Natures* (1589), and two further books of *Cantiones sacrae* (1589 and 1591). The two secular volumes were dedicated, respectively, to Sir Christopher Hatton, the lord chancellor, and to Henry Carey, 1st Baron Hunsdon, the lord chamberlain and first cousin to the queen. Both volumes of motets were dedicated to prominent Catholics: Edward Somerset, 4th earl of Worcester, a great friend and patron of Byrd's, whose loyalty to the crown was unimpeachable, and John Lumley, 1st Baron Lumley. Also in 1591 a manuscript volume of Byrd's keyboard music was prepared for "my Ladye Nevell" (probably Elizabeth, wife of Sir Henry Neville), and many more keyboard pieces found their way into the early 17th-century volume known as the *Fitzwilliam Virginal Book*, copied by another well-known Catholic, Francis Tregian, during his imprisonment in the Fleet Prison.

About 1593 Byrd moved with his family to Stondon Massey, Essex, where he lived for the rest of his life. At the accession of James I, the Catholics' prospects temporarily brightened, and this probably prompted Byrd's next three publications. In his collection of three masses and two books of *Gradualia* (1605 and 1607), he attempted to single-handedly provide a basic liturgical repertory, comprising music for the Ordinary (i.e., the unvarying parts of the mass) and for the Proper (i.e., the parts of the mass that vary according to the day or the feast) of all main feasts. It is significant that the dedicatees of both books of *Gradualia* were prominent Catholics ennobled within the first years of James's reign: Henry Howard, earl of Northampton, and John Petre, 1st Baron Petre, another close friend of Byrd's. One further publication came from Byrd, the *Psalmes, Songs and Sonnets* of 1611, containing English sacred and secular music.

LEGACY

Byrd's musical stature can hardly be overrated. He wrote extensively for every medium then available except, it seems, the lute. His virginal and organ music brought the English keyboard style to new heights and pointed the way to the achievements of other English composers, such as John Bull, Giles Farnaby, Orlando Gibbons, and Thomas Tomkins. In music for viol consort he also played an extremely important role, pioneering the development of the freely composed fantasia, which was to become the most important form of Jacobean and later composers. Although he admired Italian madrigals and as a publisher helped introduce them to England, Byrd's own secular vocal music is distinctly conservative. Much of it is conceived for the old-fashioned medium of solo voice accompanied by viol consort, which was later abandoned by the English madrigalists, with Thomas Morley (Byrd's pupil) at their head. Byrd sometimes added texts to the polyphonic accompaniments of these songs, in effect making them madrigals.

Byrd's religious beliefs did not prevent him from composing a great deal of church music to English words, most of which has survived only in manuscript. Although this is of generally high quality, it cannot be denied that

Byrd maintained his highest consistent level in his Latin sacred music. Of this, the 1589 and 1591 sets of *Cantiones sacrae* (mostly designed for the private edification of the Catholic circles Byrd moved in and therefore unrestricted by liturgical considerations) have an intensity unrivalled in England and a breadth of scale unknown on the Continent. Although the *Gradualia* are necessarily more concise and superficially more similar to the work of Giovanni Pierluigi da Palestrina and Tomás Luis de Victoria, with which Byrd was well acquainted, closer examination reveals their real individuality as well as an astonishingly consistent level of inspiration.

THOMAS MORLEY

(b. 1557/58, Norwich, Eng.—d. October 1602, London)

Thomas Morley was a composer, organist, and theorist, as well as another of the great English madrigalists. He held a number of church musical appointments, first as master of the children at Norwich Cathedral (1583–87), then by 1589 as organist at St. Giles, Cripplegate, in London, and by 1591 at St. Paul's Cathedral. In 1592 Morley was sworn in as a gentleman of the Chapel Royal.

It is highly probable that Morley converted to Roman Catholicism early in life, perhaps under the influence of his master, William Byrd. By 1591, however, Morley had defected from the church, for in that year he engaged in espionage work among the English Roman Catholics in the Netherlands.

About that time, Morley evidently began to recognize the possibilities that were offered by the new popularity of Italian madrigals fitted with English texts, for he began publishing sets of madrigals of his own composition. Morley published 25 canzonets ("little short songs," as he referred to them) for three voices in 1593. In 1597 he published 17 for five voices, and four canzonets for six voices in the same year. His first madrigals—a set of 22—appeared in 1594, and 20 ballets were published in 1595. The latter were modeled on the *balletti* of Giovanni Giacomo Gastoldi but expressed more elaborate musical development and a stronger sense of harmonic direction than Gastoldi's. Morley excelled in the lighter and more cheerful types of madrigal or canzonet.

Among his works are a considerable proportion of Italian madrigals reworked and published by Morley with no acknowledgment of the original composers—a practice not uncommon at the time. In 1598 Morley brought out a volume of English versions of selected Italian madrigals. In that same year he was granted a monopoly to print music in England for 21 years. His textbook, *A Plaine and Easie Introduction to Practicall Musicke* (1597), provides knowledge of the theoretical basis of composition of Morley's own time and that of earlier generations.

Morley's compositions are written in two distinct styles that may be chronologically separated. As a pupil of Byrd he was trained in the premadrigalian English style of broad and strong polyphony. His volumes of the 1590s, however, exhibit his mastery of Italian madrigal style and are characterized by a direct effectiveness, gentle harmonic warmth, springy rhythms, and clarity of texture.

Morley edited *The Triumphes of Oriana* (published 1603), a collection of 25 madrigals by various composers. His last volume of original compositions was *The First Booke of Ayres* (1600). Morley's body of work also includes services (primary music of the Anglican liturgy), anthems, motets, and Psalms. The six-voice motets *Laboravi in gemitu meo* and *De profundis clamavi* are considered among his best works.

JOHN DOWLAND

(b. 1562/63, Westminster, London, Eng.—d. Jan. 21, 1626, London)

A composer, virtuoso lutenist, and skilled singer, John Dowland was one of the most famous musicians of his time. Nothing is known of his childhood, but in 1580 he went to Paris as a "servant" to Sir Henry Cobham, the ambassador to the French court. In 1588 he received a bachelor of music degree from the University of Oxford. His conversion to Roman Catholicism, he believed, caused his rejection for a post as a court lutenist in 1594, and after that disappointment he left England to travel on the Continent. He visited the duke of Brunswick at Wolfenbüttel and the landgrave of Hesse at Kassel and was received with esteem at both courts. His travels also took him to Nürnberg, Genoa, Florence, and Venice, and by 1597 he had returned to England.

In 1598 Dowland became lutenist to Christian IV of Denmark, but he was dismissed for unsatisfactory conduct in 1606. Between 1609 and 1612 he entered the service of Theophilus, Lord Howard de Walden, and in 1612 he was appointed one of the "musicians for the lutes" to James I.

Although a respecter of tradition, Dowland worked during a time of musical transition and absorbed many of the new ideas he had encountered on the Continent. His 88 lute songs (printed 1597–1612) particularly reflect those influences. The early songs are presented with an alternative version for four voices. Possessing enchanting melodies, they show simple strophic settings, often in dance forms, with an almost complete absence of chromaticism. Later, in such through-composed songs as *In Darkness Let Me Dwell* (1610), *From Silent Night* (1612), and *Lasso vita mia* (1612), he introduced the Italian declamatory style, chromaticism, and dissonance; no alternative four-voice versions are given.

Dowland composed about 90 works for solo lute; many are dance forms, often with highly elaborate divisions to the repeats. His famous *Lachrimae*, or *Seaven Teares Figured in Seaven Passionate Pavans* (1604), became one of the most widely known compositions of the time. In his chromatic fantasies, the finest of which are *Forlorne Hope Fancye* and *Farewell*, he developed this form to a height of intensity unequaled by any other writer for the Renaissance lute. His compositions also include several psalm harmonizations and sacred songs printed in contemporary music books.

JOHN BULL

(b. c. 1562–63, Radnorshire, Wales?—d. March 12/13, 1628, Antwerp, Spanish Netherlands [now in Belgium])

English composer John Bull is noted for his outstanding technical ability and his virtuosity at the keyboard. Bull was educated as a chorister of the Chapel Royal in London. In December 1582 he was appointed organist and the following month choirmaster at Hereford Cathedral; but in 1585 he returned to the Chapel Royal, where in 1591 he succeeded William Blitheman, his former music teacher, as organist. Bull became a doctor of music at the universities of both Oxford and Cambridge.

In 1596 he was appointed by Elizabeth I to the professorship of music at the newly founded Gresham College in London. In 1601 he traveled in France, Germany, and the Netherlands, where his virtuosity as a keyboard player was much admired. On his return to England he continued in the royal service, and although he resigned his professorship in 1607 in order to marry, he was evidently highly

In addition to being a composer, John Bull was a keyboard virtuoso and a doctor of music at Oxford and Cambridge universities. Hulton Archive/Getty Images

esteemed at court, being named doctor of music to the king in 1612. In 1613, however, he left England and entered the service of the Archduke Albert in Brussels. Bull remained in the Netherlands, becoming in 1616 organist at the Cathedral of Antwerp.

Little of Bull's vocal music survives, and his reputation rests on his extensive compositions for virginals and organ (some 150 extant pieces), published in *Musica Britannica* (1951). His music is distinguished less by emotional depth or freshness of invention than by an unfailing resourcefulness in devising keyboard figuration. Bull combined with an essentially conservative outlook a taste for technical experiment and the solution of unusual problems—enharmonic modulations, for example, and asymmetrical rhythmic patterns. His command of the English virginalists' technique undoubtedly had an influence on his friend and contemporary J.P. Sweelinck, the Amsterdam organist, and through him on Samuel Scheidt and the north German school.

JOHN WILBYE

(baptized March 7, 1574, Diss, Norfolk, Eng.—d. September 1638, Colchester, Essex)

The madrigalist John Wilbye was the son of a successful farmer and landowner. His musical abilities early attracted the notice of the local gentry. Sir Thomas Kytson of nearby Hengrave Hall, Bury St. Edmunds, was especially interested, and he invited Wilbye to become resident musician there about 1595. The Kytsons treated him handsomely, leasing him a prosperous sheep farm in 1613; in time he came to own lands in Diss, Bury, and elsewhere. The Kytson household dissolved upon the death of Sir Thomas's widow in 1628, after which Wilbye found employment with one of Kytson's daughters in Colchester.

Wilbye's fame rests on a mere 66 madrigals, all but 2 of them published in his volumes of 1598 and 1609 (republished in volumes 6 and 7 of *The English Madrigal School*, edited by E.H. Fellowes, 1913–24, and revised by Thurston Dart, 1965–68). Wilbye's achievement lies in the grave music of his "serious" madrigals, a style then largely unpracticed in England. The "new poetry" of the Italianizing poets Sir Philip Sidney and Edmund Spenser, which flourished from 1580 to 1600, found in Wilbye's settings its perfect musical equivalent. He was far more appreciative of literary excellence in choosing texts for his music than most of his fellow madrigalists, and he also set to music many translations of Italian verse.

Wilbye spread the general emotional purport of his text (usually amorous) over the whole composition; abrupt contrasts and changes of mood were abandoned in favour of a prevailing tone, and this gave his madrigals an artistic unity rarely attained by his English contemporaries. He was a master of rhythm, and his alert ear for prosody fills his music with passages in which the verbal accent is counterpointed against the musical metre. He also experimented with sequence, recurring refrains, and thematic development in such works as "Adieu, Sweet Amaryllis" and the more complex "Draw On, Sweet Night." The latter and the well-known "Flora Gave Me Fairest Flowers" and "Sweet Honey-sucking Bees" display Wilbye's skill in vocal orchestration: the full number of voices is not kept in constant play, but for much of the time the composer writes for ever-changing smaller groups within the ensemble.

THOMAS CAMPION

(b. Feb. 12, 1567, London—d. March 1, 1620)

The multitalented Thomas Campion (Campian) was a poet, composer, musical and literary theorist, physician, and one of the outstanding songwriters of the brilliant English lutenist school of the late 16th and early 17th centuries. His lyric poetry reflects his musical abilities in its subtle mastery of rhythmic and melodic structure.

After attending the University of Cambridge (1581–84), Campion studied law in London, but he was never called to the bar. Little is known of him until 1606, by which time he had received a degree in medicine from the

AYRE

The ayre (also spelled air) is a genre of solo song with lute accompaniment that flourished in England in the late 16th and early 17th centuries. The outstanding composers in the genre were the poet and composer Thomas Campion and the lutenist John Dowland, whose *Flow, my teares (Lachrimae)* became so popular that a large number of Continental and English instrumental pieces were based on its melody. Other leading composers included John Danyel, Robert Jones, Michael Cavendish, Francis Pilkington, Philip Rosseter, and Alfonso Ferrabosco.

Ayres are typically graceful, elegant, polished, often strophic songs (i.e., songs having the same music for each stanza), dealing with amorous subjects. But many are lively and animated, full of rhythmic subtleties, while others are deeply emotional works that gain much of their effect from bold, expressive harmonies and striking melodic lines.

The ayre developed during a European trend toward accompanied solo song (in place of songs for several voices). Chansons, madrigals, and other polyphonic songs were frequently published in versions for voice and lute, and books of ayres often provided for optional performance by several singers, by having, opposite the solo and lute version, the three additional voice parts printed so that they could be read from three sides of a table.

University of Caen, France. He practiced medicine from 1606 until his death.

Campion's first publication was five sets of verses appearing anonymously in the pirated 1591 edition of

Philip Sidney's *Astrophel and Stella*. In 1595 his *Poemata* (Latin epigrams) appeared, followed in 1601 by *A Booke of Ayres* (written with Philip Rosseter), of which much of the musical accompaniment and verses were Campion's. He wrote a masque in 1607 and three more in 1613, in which year his *Two Bookes of Ayres* probably appeared. *The Third and Fourth Booke of Ayres* came out in 1617, probably followed by a treatise (undated) on counterpoint.

Campion's lyric poetry and songs for lute accompaniment are undoubtedly his works of most lasting interest. Though his theories on music are slight, he thought naturally in the modern key system, with major and minor modes, rather than in the old modal system. Campion stated his theories on rhyme in *Observations in the Art of English Poesie* (1602). In this work he attacked the use of rhymed, accentual metres, insisting instead that timing and sound duration are the fundamental element in verse structure. Campion asserted that in English verse the larger units of line and stanza provide the temporal stability within which feet and syllables may be varied.

With the exception of his classic lyric *Rose-cheekt Lawra, Come*, Campion usually did not put his advocacy of quantitative, unrhymed verse into practice. His originality as a lyric poet lies rather in his treatment of the conventional Elizabethan subject matter. Rather than using visual imagery to describe static pictures, he expresses the delights of the natural world in terms of sound, music, movement, or change. This approach and Campion's flowing but irregular verbal rhythms give freshness to hackneyed subjects and seem also to suggest an immediate personal experience of even the commonest feelings. *The Selected Songs*, edited by English-born poet W.H. Auden, was published in 1972.

FRANCIS PILKINGTON

(b. c. 1570, Lancashire?, Eng. — d. 1638, Chester, Cheshire, Eng.)

Francis Pilkington studied music extensively in his youth and received a bachelor of music degree from Lincoln College, Oxford, in 1595. He became a lay clerk at Chester Cathedral in 1602 and a minor canon 10 years later. After taking holy orders in 1614, Pilkington held various curacies in Chester as well as a rectorship in nearby Aldford. He remained involved in the Chester Cathedral choir, however, and in 1623 was named its precentor (song leader), a position he held until his death.

Despite his active career in the church, Pilkington published primarily secular compositions. *The First Booke of Songs or Ayres of 4 Parts* (1605) contains 21 songs for four voices or for solo voice and lute, as well as a pavane for lute and bass viol. While showing some influence of English composer John Dowland in their attempts at expressiveness, Pilkington's songs more closely resemble the melodic ayres of Thomas Campion and Philip Rosseter, even as their structure generally has been deemed inferior. Pilkington's shortest compositions, especially *Rest sweet nimphes*, are considered by some to be his best. The volume was dedicated to William Stanley, 6th earl of Derby, whose father and brother had served as patrons for Pilkington and his family.

Pilkington later published two sets of madrigals. Though the madrigals are not of the first rank, they are pleasing and well constructed. *The First Set of Madrigals and Pastorals of 3, 4, and 5 Parts* (1613) is rooted in the light and, at the time, somewhat antiquated style of English madrigalist Thomas Morley. The 22-piece collection notably includes a resetting of *When Oriana walkt to take the ayre*, a madrigal by Pilkington's one-time colleague Thomas Bateson (the former organist of Chester Cathedral) that paid tribute to Queen Elizabeth I. More accomplished, however, is *The Second Set of Madrigals and Pastorals of 3, 4, 5, and 6 Parts* (1624), which offers a broader range of works, including a fantasia for six viols. Particularly known among its 26 compositions are the madrigals *O softly singing lute*, for six voices, and the five-voice *Care, for thy soule*, which has been noted for its sophisticated use of chromaticism. In addition to the pieces in his three printed collections, Pilkington composed a number of solo works for lute.

THOMAS WEELKES

(baptized Oct. 25, 1576, Elsted, Sussex?, Eng.—d. Nov. 30, 1623, London)

Nothing definite is known of madrigalist Thomas Weelkes's early life, but his later career suggests that he came from southern England. He may have been the Thomas Wikes who was a chorister at Winchester College from 1583 to 1584, because he was organist there from 1598 to 1601. He was appointed organist of Chichester Cathedral probably late in 1601. He received the degree of bachelor of music at the University of Oxford in 1602, and the following year he married. In his last volume of madrigals (1608) he claimed the title "Gentleman of the Chapel Royal." From 1609 he was frequently reprimanded at Chichester for a variety of reasons, including bad language and drunkenness.

Nearly 100 of his madrigals survive, of which his finest work is in the two books of madrigals, of five and six parts, respectively, that appeared in 1600. His madrigals have been said to combine the elegance of Luca Marenzio and the firm sense of tonality characteristic of Thomas Morley with the verbal sensitivity of William Byrd. Weelkes is noted for his word painting, lively rhythms, and highly developed sense of form and structure. He also wrote music for virginal, viol, and organ. His sacred compositions, most of which were written before his appointment at Chichester in 1601, are largely unpublished. Of Weelkes's 10 Anglican services none survives complete; three that have been reconstructed blend the solo writing of the English verse anthem with the massive antiphonal style of the Venetian school. Twenty-five of Weelkes's 41 anthems are either complete or restorable; the "full" anthems (with no solo verses) show him deploying large numbers of voices. His range of expression is illustrated by the airy *balletto* in the Italian madrigal style, *On the Plains Fairy Trains* (1598). Examples of the graver manner include the madrigal *O Care, Thou Wilt Despatch Me* (1600), noted for its chromaticism (use of notes outside the basic scale, for effects of colour or intensity), and the massive anthem *O Lord, Arise*.

The madrigals of Weelkes are published in volumes 9 to 13 of *The English Madrigal School*, edited by Edmund Horace Fellowes (1913–24) and revised by Thurston Dart (1965–68).

ROBERT JOHNSON

(b. c. 1583, Eng. —d. c. 1633, London, Eng.)

English composer and lutenist Robert Johnson wrote music for a number of plays, including several by William Shakespeare, and was considered one of England's leading lutenists.

Johnson was believed to be the son of John Johnson, a composer who was also a lutenist to Elizabeth I. From 1596 to 1603 he was indentured to Sir George Carey, 2nd Lord Hunsdon, and during this time he began studying

music. He later became a court musician, serving as lutenist to James I (1604–25) and later Charles I (1625–33), and
in 1628 he was named to the post of composer for the "lute
and voices." His successor was appointed on Nov. 26, 1633,
leading modern scholars to speculate that Johnson died
shortly before that date.

About 1607 Johnson began working with the King's
Men (previously known as Chamberlain's Men), an opportunity that likely came about through his relationship
with Carey, who had earlier served as the theatrical company's patron. The troupe was closely associated with
Shakespeare, and Johnson wrote ayres (solo songs featuring lute accompaniment) for several of his plays, including
Cymbeline (1609–10) and *The Winter's Tale* (1610–11). "Full
fathom five" and "Where the bee sucks," perhaps his
best-known songs, are from *The Tempest* (c. 1611). He also
provided music for John Webster's *The Duchess of Malfi*
(c. 1612/13) and a number of plays by Francis Beaumont
and John Fletcher. Johnson's ayres, which were typically
declamatory in style, drew praise for their ability to establish character and mood. His compositions for the lute,
of which about 20 are extant, were written for the 9- or
10-course Renaissance lute and utilized the instrument's
full range. Johnson also collaborated, often with Ben
Jonson, on music for court masques, and his other works
include dances, catches, and anthems.

ORLANDO GIBBONS

(b. 1583, Oxford, Oxfordshire, Eng.—d. June 5, 1625,
Canterbury, Kent)

Orlando Gibbons was the most illustrious of a large
family of musicians that included his father, William
Gibbons (c. 1540–95), and two of his brothers, Edward and
Ellis. From 1596 to 1599 Orlando Gibbons sang in the King's

The title page from Parthenia, *which featured the virginals of Orlando* Gibbons, *as well as works by William Byrd and John Bull.* Hulton Archive/Getty Images

College Choir; he entered the University of Cambridge in 1598. In 1603 he became a member of the Chapel Royal and later became the chapel's organist, a post that he retained for the remainder of his life. In 1619 he was appointed one of the "musicians for the virginalles to attend in his highnes privie chamber," and in 1622 he was made honorary doctor of music of the University of Oxford. The following year he became organist at Westminster Abbey, where he later officiated at the funeral service of King James I. Gibbons was part of the retinue attending Charles I when the king traveled to Dover to meet his bride, Henrietta Maria, but he died shortly before her arrival from France.

Gibbons's full anthems are among his most distinguished works, as are the "little" anthems of four parts. His *Madrigals and Motetts of 5 Parts* was published in 1612. This collection contains deeply felt and very personal settings of texts that are, for the most part, of a moral or philosophical nature. It shows Gibbons's mastery of the polyphonic idiom of his day and contains many masterpieces of late madrigalist style, among them the well-known "The Silver Swan" and "What Is Our Life?" The earlier *Fantasies in Three Parts Compos'd for Viols* (c. 1610) is believed to have been the first music printed in England from engraved copperplates.

Gibbons was famous as a keyboard player, and toward the end of his life he was said to be without rival in England as an organist and virginalist. Several of his virginal pieces were published in *Parthenia* (c. 1612), and more than 40 others survive in manuscript.

CHAPTER 6

LATER RENAISSANCE COMPOSERS ACTIVE IN OTHER COUNTRIES

Composers of note could also be found in France, Germany, the Low Countries, and Spain. Typically, though not always (as Frenchman Clément Janequin illustrates), these, too, were supported by patrons, either aristocrats or churchmen.

CLÉMENT JANEQUIN

(b. c. 1485, Châtellerault, France—d. 1558, Paris)

Clément Janequin (Jannequin) worked in Bordeaux in the service of Lancelot du Fau, who became bishop of Luçon, and later for the bishop of Bordeaux. He entered the priesthood and in 1525 became canon of St. Emilion. Variously employed after 1529, when the bishop died, he was at times a student and settled in Paris in 1549. From about 1555 he was singer, and later composer, to Henry II, although not a full-time servant of the king. He died a pauper.

Although he set Psalms and composed two masses and a motet, Clément's fame lies in his 286 chansons. His program chansons—part-songs in which sounds of nature, of battles, and of the streets are imitated—include "La Bataille de Marignan" ("La Guerre"), imitating sounds of battle; "Voulez ouir les cris de Paris," with Paris street cries; and "Le Chant des oiseaux," with the sounds of birds. His style shows fine formal balance and subtle handling of texts. He is rare among great composers in that he never held an important and regular position as musician or composer to a nobleman or a bishop or archbishop.

CLAUDIN DE SERMISY

(b. c. 1490, France—d. Oct. 13, 1562, Paris)

Singer and composer Claudin (or Claude) de Sermisy, like his contemporary Clément Janequin, was one of the leading composers of chansons (part-songs). His name was associated with that of the mid-13th-century Sainte-Chapelle, Louis IX's magnificent palace chapel, as early as 1508, and in 1510 he is listed as a singer in Queen Anne of Brittany's private chapel. After her death, Sermisy is believed to have become a member of the chapel of Louis XII in 1515, and he remained in royal service under Francis I and was appointed assistant chapel master by 1533. That year he also became a canon of the Sainte-Chapelle, where he was buried in 1562.

More than half the pieces published in Pierre Attaingnant's famous collection of chansons (1529) are by Sermisy, and about 200 of Sermisy's chansons—more than 20 of which were settings of poems by his contemporary Clément Marot—were published during his life. Airy and dancelike in style, they frequently employ, with great terseness and precision, a declamatory style in which chords follow the accents of speech. Sermisy also published at least 78 motets (most for four voices), some 11 Magnificat settings, and 13 masses, as well as music for Holy Week. These sacred works are distinguishable from most other contemporary works by their privileging of text over complex musical counterpoint.

THE *GENEVAN PSALTER*

The hymnal initiated in 1539 by the French Protestant reformer and theologian John Calvin and published in a complete edition in 1562 is known as the *Genevan Psalter*. The 150 biblical Psalms were translated into French by Clément Marot and Theodore Beza and set to music by Loys Bourgeois, Claude Goudimel, and others. With the publication of this psalter in French, Calvin intended to return singing to the congregation rather than to rely upon the trained singers of a choir. The *Genevan Psalter* was soon translated into the Dutch language, and, though it had less influence on the English church, its importance to the hymnody of reformed churches throughout the world cannot be exaggerated.

LOYS BOURGEOIS

(b. c. 1510, Paris, France—d. after 1561)

Huguenot composer Loys (or Louis) Bourgeois was responsible for writing, compiling, and editing many melodic settings of Psalms in the *Genevan Psalter*. Little is known of his early life. He moved to Geneva in 1541 and lived there until 1557, when he returned to Paris. He was a friend of John Calvin and lived with him from 1545 to 1557. Bourgeois was made a citizen of Geneva in 1547. In 1551 he was imprisoned for a day for tampering with the accepted Psalm tunes without authorization, but Calvin secured his release, and eventually Bourgeois's alterations were approved.

Bourgeois based his Psalm settings on French texts by the celebrated poet Clément Marot and the leading theologian Theodore Beza. Though his harmonizations were not widely popular, the melodies he created were used by many later composers. Bourgeois used fragments of popular tunes and possibly also of liturgical chant in his melodies, the most familiar of which is *Psalm 134*, known as "Old Hundredth." He was himself responsible for about 85 melodies in the *Psalter*, which was completed by his successors in 1562. Bourgeois also wrote *Le Droict Chemin de musique* (1550; *The Direct Road to Music*) in which he proposed an adaptation of traditional solmization—using syllables to denote the tones of a musical scale.

CLAUDE GOUDIMEL

(b. c. 1514, Besançon [France]—d. Aug. 28?, 1572, Lyon)

Little is known of Claude Goudimel's early life. He was a university student in Paris in 1549 when his first chansons were published. He began working for the publisher Nicolas Du Chemin in 1551, becoming his business partner from 1552 to 1557, during which period most of Goudimel's own work was published. He set to music some of the poetry of Pierre de Ronsard. Although his early works—including five masses, three Magnificats, and several motets—reflect the Roman Catholic rite, at some point he converted to Calvinism and moved to Metz (a Huguenot city), where he lived for perhaps a decade. While in Metz he made several volumes of psalm settings, and—with Loys Bourgeois—he became an instrumental figure in the creation of the *Genevan Psalter*. Goudimel is believed to have left Metz by 1567. He worked as a music editor for the remainder of his life. He was killed in Lyon during the Massacre of St. Bartholomew's Day, which spread from Paris to the provinces.

Despite his wide range of compositions, Goudimel is remembered chiefly for his vernacular psalm settings. He completed nearly 300 Calvinist psalm settings and some 70 chansons. His first collection (1551–56) set several Psalms in the style of motets for from three to six voices. In his 1564 setting of the complete psalm cycle, the traditional melody is usually in the treble voice. The 1565 book, again a complete cycle, is written in the simplest note-against-note style, with the melody in the tenor voice. Goudimel's settings proved enormously popular, and they were widely adopted by Reformed churches.

CLAUDE LE JEUNE

(b. c. 1528/30, Valenciennes, Burgundian Hainaut [now in France]—buried Sept. 26, 1600, Paris)

Little is known of Claude Le Jeune's early life and education. As a young man he may have traveled to Venice and met the Flemish composer Adriaan Willaert, whose influence on his compositional technique is evident. In 1552 four chansons attributed to Le Jeune were included in an anthology, and in 1564 his first solo volume, *Dix pseaumes de David* ("Ten Psalms of David," in motet style), was published. By that time, Le Jeune, a Protestant, had secured the support and protection of several Huguenot nobles, which proved advantageous during the Wars of Religion, a period that extended from 1562 to 1598.

Le Jeune was centrally involved with the Academy of Poetry and Music, established in Paris in 1570 by the poet Jean-Antoine de Baïf and the musician Joachim Thibault de Courville. Following theories espoused by Pierre de Ronsard, the group sought to revive poetic forms and metres of Classical antiquity. For his part, Le Jeune created settings of *vers mesurés* (Classical-inspired French poetry) in which long and short syllables were matched by long and short note values. Although much of the academy's work was produced away from public view, some of Le Jeune's airs, with texts by Baïf, were published in 1583.

In 1581 Le Jeune contributed music to the wedding of Anne, duc de Joyeuse, to Marguerite de Lorraine-Vaudémont, the half sister of the French queen consort, Louise. By the following year Le Jeune had become choirmaster to François, duc d'Anjou, the younger brother of King Henry III. During the siege of Paris in 1590, in which Roman Catholics successfully defended the city against forces loyal to the Protestant Henry IV, Le Jeune escaped and likely took refuge at La Rochelle, where his *Dodecacorde*, a volume of 12 psalm settings, was subsequently published (1598). As the Wars of Religion waned, however, he returned to the royal court as its chamber composer.

Most of Le Jeune's work remained unseen until after his death. The majority of his hundreds of extant compositions are Psalms, including a famous series of metrical settings from the *Genevan Psalter* that was published posthumously in 1601 and was widely reprinted through the 18th century. Le Jeune's other works include airs, chansons (both sacred and secular), and canzonets. His works are noted for their skillful integration of lively rhythms with colourful melodic motifs and refined harmonies.

LUDWIG SENFL

(b. c. 1486, Basel?, Switz.—d. 1542/43, Munich, Bavaria [Germany])

Ludwig Senfl probably grew up in Zürich, and at about age 10 he joined Holy Roman Emperor Maximilian I's Hofkapelle choir. He is thought to have entered the priesthood after his voice changed, an option generally given to pubescent choirboys, and thus studied briefly on his own in Vienna, but otherwise he stayed mostly with the *Kapelle*. A pupil of Heinrich Isaac, Senfl rapidly mastered composition in the Franco-Flemish style. He collaborated with his teacher as a copyist and became chamber composer to Maximilian after Isaac's death in 1517. About that time he also started to gain international recognition for his scholarly interests in musical rhythm and poetic metre. After the emperor's death in 1519, Senfl tried without success to become a musician to Maximilian's successor, Charles V. Failing to win favour with Charles and having much difficulty receiving the payment or recognition he had been promised during Maximilian's reign, Senfl embarked on a a period of extensive travel in the early 1520s. In 1523 he settled in Munich, having obtained a post in the Hofkapelle of Duke William IV of Bavaria. He left the religious order in 1529 and took a wife, and by the following year he had begun corresponding with religious reformer Martin Luther, for whom he wrote two motets. Despite Senfl's popularity as a composer, little is known of his later life, including the date of his death.

Among Senfl's works are seven masses, which employ parody (reworking of a preexistent part-song) and cantus firmus; one mass combines two preexisting melodies simultaneously. He also composed hundreds of motets and German lieder, completed Isaac's *Choralis Constantinus* (published posthumously, 1550–55), and edited the *Liber selectarum cantionum* (1520), one of the earliest examples of German printed music.

HANS LEO HASSLER

(b. Oct. 26, 1564, Nürnberg [Germany]—d. June 8, 1612, Frankfurt am Main [Germany])

Hans Leo Hassler studied with his father, the organist Isaak Hassler (d. 1591). After mastering the imitative techniques of Orlando di Lasso and the fashionable poly-choral style of the Venetians, he traveled to Venice in 1584 to study organ playing and composition with Andrea Gabrieli. The light, elegant secular music of Orazio Vecchi, Baldassare Donato, and Giovanni Giacomo Gastoldi and the keyboard works of the Venetian school soon attracted him. In 1585 he returned to Germany as organist to the

Portrait of German composer and keyboardist Hans Leo Hassler, whose compositions fused German counterpoint and Italian form. Hulton Archive/Getty Images

LIED

The name *lied* (plural *lieder*) refers to any of a number of particular types of German song, as they are referred to in English and French writings. The earliest so-called lieder date from the 12th and 13th centuries and are the works of minnesingers, poets and singers of courtly love (*Minne*). The monophonic (single melodic line) *Minnelieder* are virile, abounding in small leaps. They are attractively contoured and make use of modal scales (melodic patterns characteristic of medieval and Renaissance music until the advent of the major–minor scale system).

The 14th century brought a decline of the monophonic lied and the introduction of polyphonic lieder for two or more voices or voice and instruments. The 15th century saw a flowering of polyphonic lieder for as many as four voices singing together. Romantic texts predominate, and through-composed pieces (i.e., devoid of sectional repetition) occur. The tunes are usually sung by the middle part (tenor); often the parts accompanying the tenor are played on instruments. The tenor melody is often a preexistent, familiar one, not a tune newly composed for the polyphonic lied. Franco-Flemish influences appear in the relations among the parts (usually three). Sometimes the texture is chordal, otherwise one part may imitate the melody of another voice for part of a phrase. When three parts are present, whether sung or played and sung, the tenor and top part (descant) form a harmonic unity, while the third part (countertenor) skips between and below the other two.

Polyphonic lieder reached a climax in the mid-16th century with the songs of Ludwig Senfl and his contemporaries. The invention of printing helped disseminate the secular polyphonic lieder, and many of the most popular ones were turned into sacred pieces by simply substituting a new text. Thus lieder became important vehicles for spreading Protestantism. By the late Renaissance (c. 1580), lieder were composed deliberately in an Italian style. Textures were often chordal, phrases were of regular length and well-articulated, and melodies were carried in the top part with the words carefully declaimed. Under the influence of the new madrigal (a polyphonic Italian secular form), the old lied tradition decayed.

Fugger banking family of Augsburg. Hassler and his brothers Kaspar and Jakob were granted titles of nobility in 1595 by Emperor Rudolf II. In 1600 he was appointed director of music for the city of Augsburg and in 1601 for Nürnberg. He moved to Dresden in 1608 to become the court organist for Christian II, elector of Saxony.

Hassler's style is a fusion of German counterpoint and Italian form. His *Madrigali* (1596), though avoiding the harmonic experiments of such 16th-century madrigalists as Luca Marenzio, are considered to be among the finest of their time. His instrumental compositions and his church music—Protestant and Roman Catholic—were widely imitated. His German songs owe much to the homophonic dance rhythms of Gastoldi. The best-known collection of these songs is the *Lustgarten* (1601; "Pleasure Garden"), which contains the charming *Mein Gemüt ist mir verwirret*. This tune reappears in Johann Sebastian Bach's *St. Matthew Passion* under the title *O Haupt voll Blut und Wunden* ("O Sacred Head Now Wounded").

CRISTÓBAL DE MORALES

(b. 1500?, Sevilla, Spain—d. between Sept. 4 and Oct. 7, 1553, Marchena?)

Cristóbal de Morales's first post was as *maestro de capilla* at the cathedral at Ávila (1526–29). After a short stay at Plasencia he joined the papal choir in Rome (1535), where he remained for 10 years, during which time he published several collections of his compositions. His work and travels with the papal choir greatly advanced his fame. During this period his health seems to have suffered, and he returned to Spain in 1545, where he was appointed *maestro de capilla* at Toledo Cathedral the same year. He left after two years, and, after a period at Marchena in the service of the duke of Arcos, he was appointed *maestro de capilla* at Málaga in 1551.

Cristóbal de Morales, engraving by James Caldwall after Angelo Rofoi, c. 1770. Hulton Archive/Getty Images

Morales's reputation continued to grow after his death. His works were published widely during his lifetime and quickly found their way to cathedrals as far away as Cuzco in Peru. The earliest printed polyphony prepared for use in the New World was Morales's 1544 book of masses, now part of the cathedral treasure of Pueblo, Mexico.

Of his 21 masses, 16 were published in Rome in 1544, under Morales's personal supervision. Morales was the first Spanish composer to write Magnificats in all eight ecclesiastical modes. They were unquestionably the most popular of his works in the 16th century and were widely reprinted. Of his many motets, the two best known are *Lamentabatur Jacob* and *Emendemus in melius*, both in five parts. His motet *Jubilate Deo omnis terra* (in six parts), commissioned by Pope Paul III to mark the peace treaty between Charles V and Francis I, was later parodied by Tomás Luis de Victoria in his mass *Gaudeamus*, and Francisco Guerrero based his mass *Sancta et immaculata* on the same motet. No less a figure than Giovanni Palestrina parodied a Morales motet for his mass *O sacrum convivium*.

ANTONIO DE CABEZÓN

(b. c. 1510, Castrillo de Matajudíos, near Burgos, Spain—d. March 26, 1566, Madrid)

Antonio de Cabezón (Cabeçon) was the earliest important Spanish composer for the keyboard. He was admired for his austere, lofty polyphonic music, which links the keyboard style of the early 1500s with the international style that emerged in the mid-16th century.

Blind from infancy, Cabezón studied organ in Palencia and in 1526 became organist and clavichordist to the empress Isabel, wife of Charles V; in 1548 he entered the service of the future Philip II. Through the court he met the influential musicians Tomás de Santa María, theorist and composer, and Luis de Narváez, the vihuelist. He traveled with the royal chapel to Italy, Germany, and the Netherlands (1548–51) and to England and the Netherlands (1554–56). His style influenced the English school of composers for the virginal and the organ style of the Low Countries exemplified by Jan Pieterszoon Sweelinck.

The bulk of Cabezón's surviving music was published in the *Libro de cifra nueva* (1557) of Luys Venegas de Henestrosa, which also contains works by other composers, and in the *Obras de música...de Antonio de Cabeçon* (1578), published posthumously by Cabezón's son Hernando. Both books are printed in *cifra nueva* ("new tablature"), a notation in which the notes of each octave are numbered 1 to 7, starting on F, with signs to indicate the particular octave; each part is printed on a single line of the staff. Both specify keyboard, lute, or vihuela (a six-course guitar tuned like the lute), although the music is clearly designed for organ or other keyboard. Hernando includes recommendations for players of the vihuela and of wind and stringed instruments.

Cabezón's compositions consist of *tientos* (ricercari, pieces often using melodic imitation); short plainsong settings for the mass and office; sets of verses on the psalm tones and their *fabordones* (i.e., *falsobordoni*, four-part chordal harmonizations of the psalm tones); a number of dance pieces; *diferencias*, or variations and divisions, on chansons and motets by the leading Continental composers and on popular song tunes; and a few vocal pieces.

His instrumental compositions are conceived for the keyboard, unusual in an era in which the style of instrumental music was taken over from vocal music. In his *tientos*, free melodic imitation gives rise to new themes. Cabezón was one of the earliest composers to use the theme-and-variations form. Especially known are his

VILLANCICO

The genre of Spanish song known as the *villancico* was most prevalent in the Renaissance but is found also in earlier and later periods. It is a poetic and musical form and was sung with or without accompanying instruments. Originally a folk song, frequently with a devotional song or love poem as text, it developed into an art music genre.

The *villancico* consisted of two parts, beginning with the refrain, or *estribillo*, which alternates with the stanza, or *copla*. The *copla* has two parts, the *mudanza* and the *vuelta*. The *vuelta* rhymes with the last line of the *mudanza* but is sung to the melody of the *estribillo*. This overlap of poetic and musical form is characteristic of the *villancico*.

The *villancico* repertory of the late 15th–early 16th centuries is found in several *cancioneros*, or song collections. The pieces were in three or four voice parts, the musical texture being either homophonic (chordal) or contrapuntal. An important composer was Juan del Encina. Around 1500, settings of *villancico*s as solo songs accompanied by *vihuela*, a guitar-shaped lute, appeared, some in Portuguese as well as Spanish. Composers included some of the great masters of the *vihuela*, such as Luis Milán and Miguel de Fuenllana.

variations on the song "Canto del caballero" and the three sets of variations on "Guárdame las vacas."

FRANCISCO GUERRERO

(b. Oct. 4?, 1528, Sevilla, Spain—d. Nov. 8, 1599, Sevilla)

Francisco Guerrero was a choirboy in Sevilla (Seville) and at age 18 became chapelmaster at Jaén Cathedral in Andalusia, Spain. In 1546 he was appointed cantor at Sevilla Cathedral, assuming effective musical directorship in 1551 and becoming chapelmaster in 1574. Except for a trip to Rome and one to Jerusalem, he spent most of his working life in Sevilla. Guerrero's music is considered eminently vocal, strongly Spanish in character, and evocative of a vivid and serene spirituality. His compositions include instrumental music for *vihuela*, 19 masses, 2 requiems, settings of the Passions of St. Matthew and St. John, Latin motets, and sacred songs in Spanish.

ADRIAAN WILLAERT

(b. c. 1490, Bruges, Flanders?—d. Dec. 8, 1562, Venice [Italy])

Flemish composer Adriaan Willaert contributed significantly to the development of the Italian madrigal and helped establish Venice as one of the most influential musical centres of the 16th century.

Willaert studied law at the University of Paris but abandoned this in favour of music, studying with the composer Jean Mouton. In 1527 he became music director of St. Mark's, Venice, where he created a school that attracted musicians from all over Europe. His students included Cipriano de Rore, Gioseffo Zarlino, and Andrea Gabrieli.

Willaert's madrigals show a gradual synthesis of the contrapuntal style of the Franco-Flemish school and the growing Italian emphasis on harmonic colour and expressiveness. His chansons reflect a similar development. As a composer of sacred music he is known primarily for his motets. Probably inspired by the two opposing choir lofts at St. Mark's, he developed a style of polyphony in which two four-part choirs sing alternately, but occasionally combine in an eight-part section. This led directly to the polychoral writing that characterized Venetian music in the second half of the 16th century. Willaert was also one of the earliest composers to write purely instrumental works: canzoni, ricercari, and fantasies for organ and for instrumental ensembles.

NICOLAS GOMBERT

(b. c. 1490, southern Flanders [now in Belgium]—d. c. 1556, Tournai, Flanders)

Nicolas Gombert traveled widely as a singer and master of the choirboys in the Chapel Royal of Charles V and later held positions at the cathedrals of Courtrai and Tournai. Like Josquin des Prez, he developed techniques of melodic imitation, but Gombert used a freer, less symmetrical style. His compositions are smooth and even in texture, with less dramatic feeling than those of Josquin. His musical textures and his unobtrusive handling of dissonance point to the later style of Palestrina. His chansons are admired for their fresh, straightforward quality.

Gombert was viewed by his colleagues as an innovator. In his travels he was influential in spreading the Franco-Flemish style that dominated the Renaissance. His works include about 160 motets, about 60 chansons, 10 masses, and eight Magnificats.

JACOBUS CLEMENS

(b. c. 1510, Ieper, Burgundian Flanders—d. c. 1556, Diksmuide, Spanish Netherlands)

In 1544 Jacobus Clemens (Clement) was probationary choirmaster of Saint-Donatien in Brugge (Bruges), and in 1550 he was a singer and composer at 's-Hertogenbosch (now in the Netherlands). An elegy of 1558 suggests that he died violently. His outstanding *Souter Liedekens* (1556) was an almost complete series of metrical Psalms in Flemish. His other works include 16 masses, more than 200 motets, and 90 chansons. He used simple, impressive themes, melodious lines, and skillful melodic imitation.

JAN PIETERSZOON SWEELINCK

(b. April 1562, Amsterdam—d. Oct. 16, 1621, Amsterdam)

Jan Pieterszoon Sweelinck succeeded his father as organist of the Oude Kerk (Old Church), Amsterdam, in about 1580 and remained in this post until his death. Apparently he never left the Low Countries and traveled only to Rotterdam and Antwerp.

Although he composed much sacred and secular vocal music in the polyphonic traditions of France and the Netherlands (including the chansons, the *cantiones sacrae*, and settings of the Psalms), Sweelinck was chiefly known as an organist and keyboard composer. His keyboard music includes chorale variations, toccatas and fantasias showing the influence of the Venetian organ school, and sets of variations on secular tunes.

Sweelinck's fantasias are among the first organ fugues in which a single theme is subjected to augmentation, diminution, and changes of rhythm and combined with counterthemes. His secular variations drew upon popular tunes of several European countries; an example is the set of variations on *Mein junges Leben hat ein End'*.

It is possible that Sweelinck met the English composers John Bull and Peter Philips during their visits to the Low Countries; Bull's "Fantasia on a Theme of Sweelinck" was the tribute of one keyboard virtuoso to another. Sweelinck's keyboard playing was widely known. His

Portrait of Jan Pieterszoon Sweelinck. The Dutch composer's technique was passed on to generations of organists across Europe, including George Frideric Handel and Johann Sebastian Bach. Hulton Archive/ Getty Images

organ pupils included the German composers Samuel Scheidt and Heinrich Scheidemann; Scheidemann's pupil J.A. Reinken handed on this tradition of organ playing to the Danish organist Dietrich Buxtehude. Many outstanding organists of the following generation, particularly in northern Germany, were pupils of Sweelinck; Handel and Bach were influenced by this northern German school of organ playing.

CONCLUSION

In music, as well as many other spheres, the Renaissance was a time of great change in the Western world. The amalgamation of Northern (Netherlandish) and Southern (mostly Italian) techniques culminated in the work of Josquin des Prez. In his works the elaborate polyphony of the north and the chordal, harmonically controlled style of the south are fused into a rich and expressive language—the perfect union of words and music.

In addition to polyphony, a major feature of Renaissance music was the emancipation of instrumental from vocal music. The two- and three-part music of the 13th century developed into a norm of four parts in the art music of the 15th century, and to five or six parts by the middle of the 16th. These parts could be and were taken by a variety of vocal and instrumental combinations. Performers included members of consorts, instrumental ensembles that could be either "whole" (i.e., using instruments from one family of strings or winds) or "broken" (using instruments from more than one family).

Polyphony manifested itself on all musical fronts. In sacred music, notably the motet and the mass, modal counterpoint was paramount, probably because of its close kinship with the traditional sound of liturgical plainchant. In secular music polyphony took the form of functional harmony developed in the French chanson, the Italian madrigal, and related types. Undisturbed by the theoretical writings from the pens of church-employed musicians, secular musical practice in the later Renaissance laid the foundations for the harmonic notions that were to dominate more than three centuries of Western art music.

GLOSSARY

ayre A type of song sung with lute accompaniment popular in England during the Renaissance.

ballad A narrative composition in rhythmic verse suitable for singing.

bow In music, a wooden rod, usually having horsehairs stretched end to end, that is used in playing stringed instruments such as those of the viol or violin family.

canon A musical form and compositional technique based on the principle of strict imitation.

chant In music, a type of song marked by rhythmic repetition.

codify To classify or systematize.

contrapuntal Employing counterpoint, which is when one or more independent melodies added above or below a given melody.

diatonic Relating to a musical scale comprising intervals of five whole steps and two half steps.

fantasia A free-flowing musical composition that does not adhere to a strict form.

fingerboard The section of a stringed instrument against which the player's fingers press the strings to change a string's pitch.

motet A polyphonic choral composition on a sacred text usually without instrumental accompaniment.

notation A system of symbols that, in music, represent notes of a song, their duration, and the key in which they are to be sounded, among other things.

pitch The property of a sound, especially a musical tone, that determines how high or low the sound is.

plainsong A simple, monophonic melody free of specific rhythm, typically sung as part of a Christian religious service; a Gregorian chant.

polyphony The blending of two or more independent melodies into a single harmonic texture.

psalmody The act of singing psalms (sacred, poetic scriptural text) in the course of worship.

recitative A style of vocal music wherein the singer imitates the natural inflections of speech; used for dialogue and narrative in operas and oratorios.

repertory A slate of musical selections available for performance.

staff The horizontal lines with their spaces on which musical notes are written.

timbre The quality of tone distinctive of a particular singing voice or musical instrument.

tone A sound of definite pitch and vibration.

treble The upper half of the whole vocal or instrumental tonal range, the lower half being bass.

troubadour A lyric poet, sometimes of knightly rank, who sang poems whose major theme was courtly love.

virtuoso One who excels in the technique of an art; especially a highly skilled musician.

BIBLIOGRAPHY

Survey histories that set the music of the Renaissance period in context and include substantial sections on the Renaissance are J. Peter Burkholder, Donald Jay Grout, and Claude V. Palisca, *A History of Western Music*, 8th ed. (2010); Barbara Russano Hanning and Donald Jay Grout, *Concise History of Western Music*, 4th ed. (2010); Thomas Forrest Kelly, *Early Music: A Very Short Introduction* (2011); K. Marie Stolba, *The Development of Western Music: A History*, 3rd ed. (1998).

Books that treat only the Renaissance period are Leeman L. Perkins, *Music in the Age of the Renaissance* (1999); Allan W. Atlas, *Renaissance Music: Music in Western Europe, 1400–1600* (1998); Howard Mayer Brown and Louise K. Stein, *Music in the Renaissance*, 2nd ed. (1999).

More specialized books include Fiona Kisby (ed.), *Music and Musicians in Renaissance Cities and Towns* (2001), an interdisciplinary treatment that includes the work of urban historians and musicologists; Jeffery T. Kite-Powell (ed.), *A Performer's Guide to Renaissance Music*, 2nd ed., revised and expanded (2007); and Jeremy L. Smith, *Thomas East and Music Publishing in Renaissance England* (2003). Lewis Lockwood, *Music in Renaissance Ferrara 1400–1505: The Creation of a Musical Center in the Fifteenth Century*, rev. ed. (2009); and Paul Merkley and Lora L.M. Merkley, *Music and Patronage in the Sforza Court* (1999), examine the period from the perspective of two noted Italian centres of musical development, Ferrara and Milan. Dolores Pesce (ed.), *Hearing the Motet: Essays on the Motet of the Middle Ages and Renaissance* (1998), treats the nature of that highly significant vocal genre. Volumes such as Matthew Spring, *The Lute in Britain* (2001); and Alexander Silbiger (ed.),

Keyboard Music Before 1700, 2nd ed. (2004), treat individual instruments. Richard Sherr (ed.), *The Josquin Companion* (2000); David Fallows, *Josquin* (2009); and Glenn Watkins, *Gesualdo: The Man and His Music*, 2nd ed. (1991), and *The Gesualdo Hex: Music, Myth, and Memory* (2010), are among many works that discuss the lives and music of individual Renaissance composers.

INDEX

A

Adam de La Halle, 12
allemande, 19
Ambrosian chant, 2
Arcadelt, Jacques, 25, 67–69
Ars Antiqua, 8, 9–10, 16
Ars cantus mensurabilis ("The Art of Measured Song"), 9
Ars Nova, 8–10, 13, 16
Attaingnant, Pierre, 66, 78–79, 126
ayres, 26, 117, 122

B

Bach, J.S., 20, 63, 86, 134, 143
ballades, 13, 16, 51, 52, 53, 62
ballade style, 16
Ballard family, 79
ballatas, 10
ballettos, 26
basse danse, 19
Binchois, 14, 49, 54–55
Bourgeois, Loys, 127–128
Bull, John, 22, 23, 105, 109, 113–115, 141
Burgundy, court of, 14–15, 54
Buxheimer Orgelbuch, 18
Buxtehude, Dietrich, 20
Byrd, William, 23, 26, 61, 70, 79, 102, 103, 104, 105, 106–110, 111, 121

C

Cabezón, Antonio de, 22, 136–139
caccias, 10
Campion, Thomas, 26, 116–118, 119
cantus firmus, 8, 15, 21–22, 24, 27, 50, 53, 58, 60, 63, 84, 85
canzona, 19, 21
canzonetta, 26, 74, 110, 111, 130
chansons, 15, 21, 27, 51–52, 54, 55, 57, 58, 60, 62, 64, 67, 69, 70, 73, 78, 117, 125, 126, 128, 129, 130, 137, 140, 141, 144
clavichord, 23, 39–40, 40–42
Clemens, Jacobus, 141
Compère, Loyset, 63–64, 78
conductus, 8
cornetto, 48
counterpoint, 61–62, 86, 87, 100, 116, 134
courante, 19
crumhorn, 46–47
curtal, 47, 48

D

Dowland, John, 22, 26, 31, 112–113, 117, 119
Dufay, Guillaume, 14–15, 16, 49, 50–54, 57
Dunstable, John, 14, 49–50, 54, 57

E

East, Thomas, 79
eschiquier, 39
estampie, 13

F

familiar style, 17
fantasias, 19, 31, 41, 109, 141
Farnaby, Giles, 105, 109
fauxbourdon, 52
Fayrfax, Robert, 100–101
Fitzwilliam Virginal Book, 105, 108
flutes, 45–46
Franco-Flemish school, 16–18
Franco of Cologne, 9
Frescobaldi, Girolamo, 20
Froberger, Johann Jakob, 20
frottola/frottole, 25, 26, 63, 64, 68, 69, 78
Fundamentum organisandi (*Fundamentals of Organ Playing*), 18

G

Gabrieli, Andrea, 22, 23, 25, 87–88, 132, 139
Gabrieli, Giovanni, 20, 25, 87, 88–89, 95
galliard, 19
Gaukler, 12
Genevan Psalter, 127, 128, 130
Gesualdo, Carlo, principe di Venosa, 26, 75–80
Ghirardello da Firenze, 10
Gibbons, Orlando, 23, 26, 102, 109, 122–124
Giovanni da Cascia, 10

gleemen, 12
Gombert, Nicolas, 60, 140
Goudimel, Claude, 79, 127, 128–129
Gregorian chant, 3
Guerrero, Francisco, 136, 139
Guido d'Arezzo, 4, 5–6
Guidonian hand, 5

H

harpsichord, 23, 33, 39, 42, 43, 44
Hassler, Hans Leo, 27, 75, 88, 131–134

I

imitation, 17, 20, 21, 61, 66
instrumental music
    evolution of, 18
    musical forms, 19–22
    solo and ensemble instruments, 22–23
intonazione, 19
Isaac, Heinrich, 27, 62–63, 131

J

Jacopo da Bologna, 10
Janequin, Clément, 27, 79, 125–126
Johnson, Robert, 121–122
jongleurs, 12
Josquin des Prez, 17, 51, 55, 58–62, 64, 65, 78, 92, 140, 143

K

King's Hunt, The, 19

L

Landini, Francisco, 10
La Rue, Pierre de, 64–65
Lasso, Orlando di, 27, 52, 61, 62, 71–73, 79, 87, 88, 132
Le Jeune, Claude, 129–130
Léonin, 6, 9
lied/lieder, 27, 63, 73, 131, 133–134
Lorenzo da Firenze, 10
lute, 20, 22, 26, 28–31, 33, 34, 52, 109, 112, 113, 117, 118, 119, 120, 122, 137, 138

M

Machaut, Guillaume de, 13, 15, 51
madrigals, development of, 25–26
Magnus Liber Organi ("Great Book of Organum"), 6
Marenzio, Luca, 26, 74–75, 89, 120, 134
mass, growing importance of as musical form, 15
Meistersingers, 12
Merulo, Claudio, 20
Micrologus, 4
Milán, Luis, 22, 31
minnesingers, 12
minstrels, 12
Monte, Philippe de, 25, 69–71
Monteverdi, Claudio, 26, 74, 75, 89–99
Morales, Cristóbal de, 134–136
Morley, Thomas, 26, 74, 79, 109, 110–111, 119, 120
motet, explanation and rise of, 8, 9–10, 15, 24
Mouton, Jean, 65–66

Musica enchiriadis, 4
musical/staff notation, 5–6, 9
musique mesurée, 27

N

Netherlands school, 16
Notker Balbulus, 3
Notre-Dame school, 6–8

O

Obrecht, Jakob, 17, 57–58
Ockeghem, Jean de, 17, 55–57, 61, 78
opera, 89, 93, 94, 98, 99
organ, 19, 20, 21, 22, 37–38, 80, 87, 89, 106, 109, 114, 121, 131, 136, 137, 140, 141, 143
organum, 4, 6
organum purum, 6

P

Palestrina, Giovanni Pierluigi da, 53, 61, 62, 69, 70, 72, 74, 80–87, 92, 140
Paris motet, 8
parody technique, 85
Paumann, Conrad, 18
pavane, 19
percussion instruments, 35–36
Pérotin, 6, 9
Petrucci, Ottaviano dei, 78
Pierre de la Croix, 9
Pilkington, Francis, 117, 119–120
polyphony, development of, 3–6
Praetorius, Michael, 28, 36
preludes, 19, 23

printers, music, 78–79, 104, 107
printing, invention and
    development of, 16, 24, 78–79
psaltery, 43

R

rackett, 47
rebec, 33
recorders, 45
ricercar, 19
rondeaux, 13, 15, 51, 52, 62

S

Sachs, Hans, 12
sackbut, 48
scops, 12
Senfl, Ludwig, 27, 63, 130–131, 133
Sermisy, Claudin de, 27, 126
serpent, 46
shawms, 23, 28, 47, 48
solmization, 5, 128
sordone, 47
spinet, 23, 39, 42–44
Sweelinck, Jan Pieterszoon, 115,
    137, 141–143

T

Tallis, Thomas, 79, 102, 103–106,
    107, 108
Taverner, John, 101–102
Terminorum musicae diffinitorium, 18
theorbo, 31–33
Tinctoris, Johannes, 18

toccatas, 19, 20, 23, 142
Tomkins, Thomas, 109
tourdion, 19
tropes/troping, 3
troubadours, 12, 51
trouvères, 12, 51
Tuotilo, 3
Tye, Christopher, 102–103

V

villancico, 27, 138
villanelles, 26, 75
viols, 23, 28, 33–37, 109, 119,
    120, 121
*virelai*s, 13, 15, 51, 52
virginals, 23, 39, 44–45, 105, 106,
    109, 114, 121, 124, 137
Vitry, Philippe de, 8
vocal music, Renaissance, 22–25
    England, 26
    France, 27
    Germany and other areas of
        Europe, 27
    Italy, 25–26

W

Walther von der Vogelweide, 12
Weelkes, Thomas, 26, 79,
    120–121
Wert, Giaches de, 73–74, 91, 92
Wilbye, John, 26, 79, 115–116
Willaert, Adriaan, 25, 65, 129,
    139–140

3 1170 00935 8346